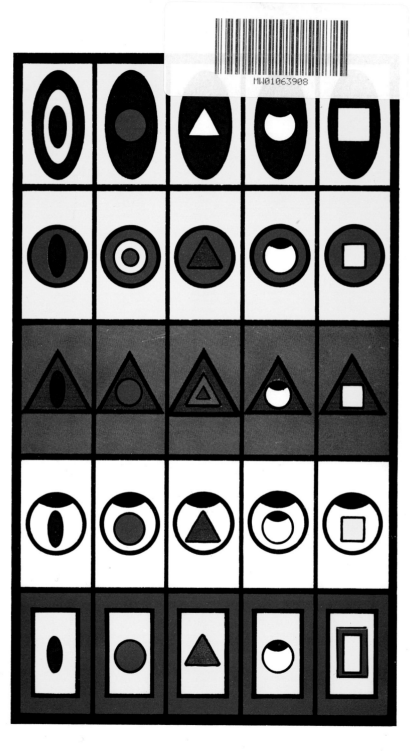

Water of Air

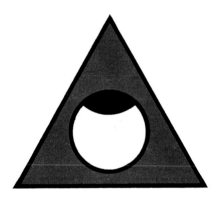

Water of Fire

Water of Water

73

Air of Air

Air of Fire

Air of Water

Air of Earth

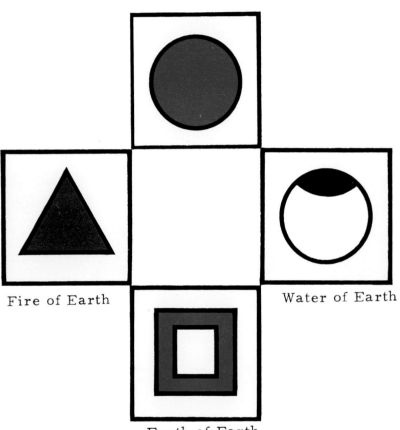

Fire of Earth

Water of Earth

Earth of Earth

Fire of Air

Fire of Fire

Fire of Water

88

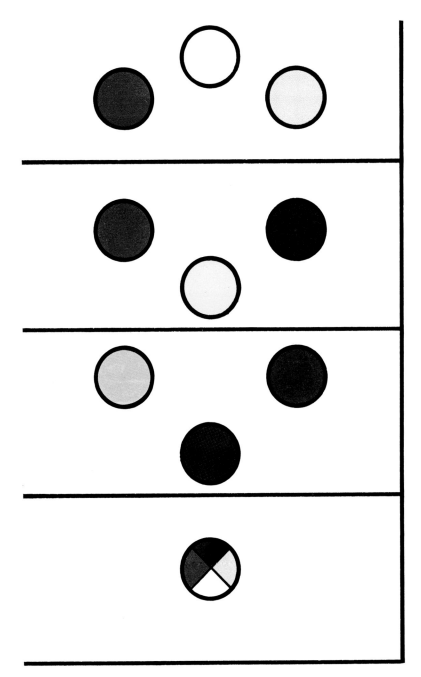

Fig. 1a

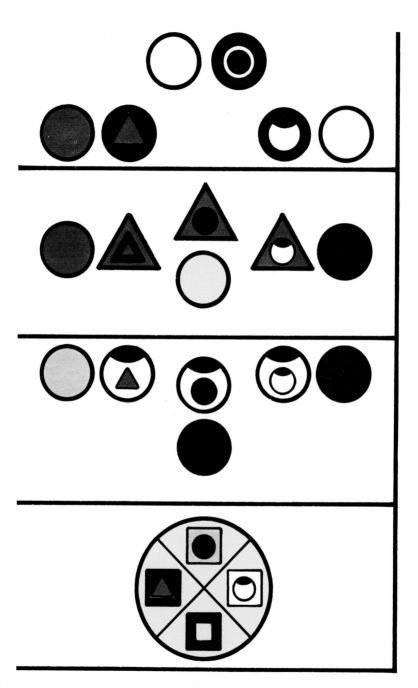

Fig. 2a

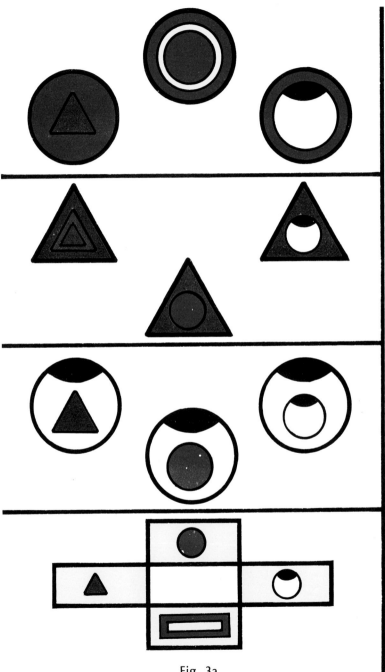

Fig. 3a

THE ART AND PRACTICE OF CABALLA MAGIC

THE ART AND PRACTICE OF CABALLA MAGIC
by
OPHIEL

AUTHOR OF

The Art and Practice of Astral Projection
*

The Art and Practice of Getting
Material Things Through Creative Visualization
*

The Art and Practice of the Occult
*

The Art and Practice of Clairvoyance
*

The Oracle of Fortuna
*

The Art and Practice of Talismanic Magic
AND
"Occult Vignettes"

SAMUEL WEISER, INC.
New York

First Published by Edward C. Peach 1976

First Published in 1977

Samuel Weiser, Inc.
740 Broadway
New York, N.Y. 10003

ISBN 0-87728-303-6

Printed in the USA by
NOBLE OFFSET PRINTERS, INC.
NEW YORK

DEDICATION

To my students of the future — Hello!!

For a large number of reasons, not the least the personality of Ophiel, today is not seeing the wide distribution of these books. Ophiel jokingly, although his heart is cracking up (more than one way), accuses others of allowing the Devil to fuddle up their minds so as to prevent this book from coming out, or, now that it is out, to slow down its distribution, as well as the distribution of the other books, to prevent Truth from being known and used.

Oh well, into each life some rain must fall. (but does it have to be a permanent flood?) I'll keep on going. Drops of water can wear away the hardest stone, in time! So mote it be!

Ophiel
West Hollywood, California
Spring 1976

Please note that in this edition color plates of the diagrams referred to in Chapters 3 and 4 appear at the beginning of the book.

TABLE OF CONTENTS

Introduction and Foreword

This World Plane presents confusion compounded upon confusion to the seeking student of the Occult (who really "lives" on all planes at once).

On every side, and also down from above and up from below, come all kinds of "screams" of supposed authentic knowledge — Information (is there a difference?) about what is what in/of the Occult, the voices of teachers and masters (?), revelations of "leaders" demanding instant obedience and obeisance to themselves, and dire threats if instant submission is not forthcoming at once. And so on far into the night — enough to drive any sincere Occult student mad with confusion (oh, I said that before!).

As I have taken to saying lately, the study of the Occult is full of blinds, dead ends and traps for the student. IF HE CANNOT THINK HIS WAY OUT OF THESE BLINDS, DEAD ENDS, AND TRAPS HE WILL REMAIN FOREVER CAUGHT THEREIN AT SOME SPOT, AND NO FURTHER PROGRESS WILL BE POSSIBLE UNTIL HE RELEASES HIMSELF BY PROGRESSIVE ATTAINMENT, THINKING OF WHAT IS TRUE.

It is true that Truth is relative, and, in the case of individuals, accumulative. However, the increasing accumulation of additional Truth Knowledge should not be at variance with the first early Truth Knowledge. Additional Knowledge should be an expansion of the first Knowledge, and so on.

Truth about what? First, as much accurate Truth as can be acquired about the nature of God. Second, as much accurate Truth as can be acquired about the nature of the Physical Universe and the Inner Planes thereof (which Inner

1

Planes are really physical, too). Third, as much accurate Truth as can be acquired about you — yourself, your possible powers, their use, and expanded use, and continued expanded use.

There exists an Occult system of Truth Knowledge called the Caballa (there are a number of different ways of writing this word: Cabala, Caballah, Qabalah, all mean the same thing). The Caballa system has many advantages over any other system I have ever heard of in the matter of immediate accurate Truth Knowledge, but to my mind vastly more important is the fact that in this system you can *grow* in *Knowledge* and *Power*, at your own pace, and NEVER REACH AN END. No matter how much Knowledge, Truth, and Power you "get" there is forever a thousand million times more Knowledge and Power ahead with, as I said, no possible end in sight.

Some basic description of the Caballa system is in order here now.

First — there is the historical background of this system, not too much of which is known as the system was always held by its followers to be very secret; what was written down was incomplete, and the incomplete parts were never written down (they didn't have to be for when a person acquired a definite portion on the Caballa Knowledge, he then *knew* the missing parts intuitively, and so will you!).

As an aside, it appears that the Muslim religion in the 13th-15th centuries was not as straightlaced as the hidebound Christians were, and it appears that they dealt freely and openly with the Inner Worlds — Planes — Matters of the Caballa — as well as invocations and evocations to all kinds of "Spirits," good and otherwise, and in fact I am told, taught these things in their universities in Spain before the insane Ferdinand and Isabella drove them out in 1491.

But before the Moors took up the Caballa, in point of fact, before the Jews existed as a Palestine nation, before Babylon in Egypt, some form of the Caballa existed *because* all the Gods and Goddesses of any nation, at any time, at any place, ALL FIT ON TO THE CABALLA PATTERN, and this does not seem to be an accident.

Second — there is the "structure" pattern of the Caballa glyph, called the Tree of Life, and how *you* fit into this pattern, and how the Pattern allows for the life pattern of all of us, by embracing and demonstrating our lives, the past, the present and the future, thus presenting us with the key to Power over our Life.

Third — there is the attachment of all Forces to the Tree of Life Pattern glyph and what this means to you in terms of how you can USE the FORCES that constitute the Physical Cosmos for your benefit and not allow them to use you for your detriment. This is done through Knowledge.

Fourth — additional control over your life living is gained through Knowledge that all physical things, institutions, objects are attached or, as Dion Fortune says, filed under the headings of the various Sephiroth. Thus when you are working or going to work with a certain definite subject, you can look at the subject's position on the Tree of Life glyph and determine at once the Forces (Gods) that rule that subject and how best to work with it, because you then know what its basic nature is, as well as the basic nature of the forces that "rule" that subject.

Fifth — my researches have shown, to my satisfaction, that the Physical Cosmos Universe consists of Five Elemental Forces, and their combinations, and practically nothing else, as is shown by the Caballa pattern layout.

These Five Elemental Forces, and their combinations, are irretrievably connected to the Tree of Life, and this fact has not been actively demonstrated, to my knowledge, by anyone before, or its significance explained. A whole new world opened up for me when I realized this. I hope it does for you.

The object of all my writings is to make our lives better through Knowledge and Understanding of, let us say, "divine things." So here is another book, an Occult book, for your benefit and advancement. This book is a part of a forthcoming series which I hope will continue to grow for as long as I am able to hold a pen.

Since starting to write this book, I have been reading a very interesting and profound book about the history of the Golden Dawn type of secret societies, and some biographical material about some of the people involved in these societies from the year 1880 up until now.

The author, in referring to Dion Fortune and her writings, says, "Dion Fortune's occult books and articles . . . *most of these were rather vulgar pot-boiling journalism.*" (italics mine).

I thought her books were quite good, and by no stretch of verbilization would I have called her writings vulgar or pot-boiling.

So I am now wondering, what are my books called, or going to be called!

Well, I'm sorry, dear Occult students, the writing I do is the best that I want to do. As I said before, I know my books are not glorious literature, but, while I suppose I'd like to write glorious literature, I am trying to write/teach the Occult and that subject is quite different.

Don't get the idea, dear students, that I think my books and writings are "pot boilers." I DO NOT SO THINK. Naturally, I think my books are wonderful. I *do* write a little loose and apparently non-classic, but that is to present the subject instead of a glorious style of writing, so you don't get distracted from the Occult material.

There are a number of announcements in the back of this book which I trust will be of interest to you. Please read and consider them carefully.

OPHIEL
Hollywood, 1975

Post Script — As I start the, to me, agonizing job of getting this book ready for the printer I am reading it for the first time in a month, and I am struck by my references to KNOWLEDGE as a means of power ESCAPE from this WORLD or rather as a means of CONTROL over the tur-

4

bulent disorganized Forces with which we now have to contend all our lives. DO NOT NEGLECT THIS BOOK, BUT THE NEXT BOOK IS ABOUT KNOWLEDGE which the Greeks called THE GNOSIS WHICH CAN HELP YOU ON YOUR WAY THROUGH THIS OUTER PHYSICAL WORLD AND INTO WHAT YOU ARE LOOKING FOR.

Additional Foreword

It has occurred to me in getting this different book ready for the press that someone is going to step up and say to me, "How have you put all these things into use/practice yourself, and as you apparently have not done so, or if you did they didn't work, hence they are no good, etc., etc."

No one regrets this more than me, that I don't stop, STOP the seeking of new things and giving them out to you, but instead retire to some secluded spot and seek out the higher/deeper Occult Knowledge *for my own use*, and then USE it myself, and stop all this teaching.

Well! I can't do it! I seem to be compelled to seek and publish, albeit somewhat slowly.

You students out there are going to USE this material *for your benefit much better than I'll use it for my benefit.* You'll get more out of this than I will.

I think my books will last long after I am gone, and others benefit from them much more than I will. And all I will have is fame (such is life).

To the Critics: I don't understand the critics' reason for being critics. I didn't write the Ophiel books for the critics. I wrote them to "help" (poorest damned excuse in existence) "others" (?). I certainly didn't write them to make money, as I have made none to speak of. Others have chiseled me out of the money, and I have been left with the glory, which is now and then blasted by the critics.

I don't mind criticism if I learn something from it, but of the criticism that has turned up so far I have a very definite double feeling: (1) The critics didn't read the book

5

thoroughly and completely, and (2) the critics didn't understand the material in the book while reading it.

And, the reason they didn't understand the material is that they weren't capable of understanding the material in the first place. It was quite clear to me that the critics didn't have the inner perception of the Occult so as to be capable of properly evaluating my book/books. So what the hell good was the criticism, except to show up their ignorance?

I would gladly welcome some deep thoughts that would show/lead me into another forward view that I had missed, or not reached, but none of the criticisms were like that at all; most of them were carping cracks about my "style," how my style is irritating, and such bull as that. In one of my books I made a statement/reference to the Elemental Force of Water, and to the fact that the Great Lakes had fallen in their levels, and suggested a connecting remedy, which passed entirely over the head of one Critic, who saw no connection whatsoever. In his ensuing remarks he only revealed his abysmal ignorance of the Occult. By the way, what connection *could* there be between the water level in the Great Lakes, and the Elemental Force of Water? Or, how could Nature be helped to restore the Great Lakes, by YOUR knowledge of the Elemental Force of Water?*

The only type of person who is capable of reviewing my occult books is a person like Dr. Francis Israel Regardie, and he is too busy to do it. So, unless you've got plenty on the occult ball don't make a fool out of yourself by trying to review my books. If you want to do a good job of reviewing and criticizing, then follow the directions and *develop yourself,* and talk about that and forget the other, which is nothing.

---

*When these statements were written, the Great Lakes were low. I saw in a magazine article recently that the Great Lakes are full again and overflowing, and, incidentally, causing a great deal of damage. So Nature does correct herself and does go in cycles which idea-fact of cycles I commend to your most careful consideration and attention, for now and for the future.

As I am about to give this book over to the printer I am beset by an anxious feeling that this book is not going to be an entertaining book to read for amusement, or to pass an idle hour! This book is about a very different subject than ordinary life, and hence my organization of the materials is not ordinary quickie stuff. Please treat the material in this book as not-of-this-world-familiar-Knowledge. Follow the study as it unfolds, and don't look for instant connections!!!

Ophiel
West Hollywood, California 1976

Chapter 1

What History of the Caballa is available.

For those who have found my books for the first time (to old readers I apologize for repetitions):

To my dear new occult student readers: I am an informal person. I do not believe in substituting a stiff literary formality, or a "canned" lecture talk, for achievability in the Occult Arts. I am not like any of the other occult teachers, in that I am not telling you what wonderful *natural* occult *gifts* I had given to me (by God?), and therefore you must come and follow me blindly, and throw all your material possessions at my feet, and buy meditation robes from me at $150 a robe, as some Swami is doing, or buy other occult sundries such as Akashic record readings for $250 or a *lesser* Akashic record of past lives reading for $150. No, I have none of these things available, just Occult Knowledge teaching and practices which YOU have to learn and do, yourselves, for your own benefit.

Also, dear students, the study of the Occult is not hard. BUT the study of the Occult is DIFFERENT, much different from any other earth plane study, and, unhappy as it may sound to you, I have found that the only really dependable manner in which I can convey these great and noble truths to your consciousness so they catch on, is through repetition which I do with important points throughout the book several times if I think/feel it is necessary to get the idea over. When you come to a repetition, then please consider that the repetition is not there to pad out the book but to emphasize an important point of Occult Knowledge which please make your own and study all over again. (The repetitions infuriate critics, but I am not

9

writing glorious literature to *entertain* the critics but to teach a different kind of Knowledge; if I could do it a better way I would, or if I knew someone who did it better, I'd send you to him).

I may occasionally say in this book, and in my lectures, that I don't know. When you hear me say I don't know, or read this, don't get any ideas that I am denigrating myself. Oh, no, not at all. When I say, "I don't know," I also mean that to the best of my knowledge no one else knows (really knows), so don't let it throw you.

In the following pages I am going to give you several different kinds of examples of religious types of thinking. Please read them over carefully, making mental notes about how far apart these ideas are in time and space (a favorite expression of mine), but how they have similar basic ideas at the base/bottom of each.

I have covered some different ground here, and the critics are not going to like it, concerned as they are with their preconceived ideas of formality. I wanted you to have a quick picture of widely different religious ideas, I repeat, so get that out of the material following.

With these observations out of the way, we can now proceed.

In the case of the subject of this section, the History of the Caballa, there is no *real* definitive history of the Caballa to give! As was said before not only was the Caballa Tree of Life diagram not drawn nor the explanation written down in ancient times, but, on top of that, so few people could read and write that it wouldn't have helped much if it had been written down completely and handed out to the mobs everywhere!

You would have expected that Dion Fortune would have given some connected reliable history about the beginnings of the Caballa system, but she gives very little information.

On page 3 of her book *The Mystical Qabalah* (note her spelling of the word), Dion Fortune intimates that, due to the fact that Abraham and Joseph went to Egypt (so did

Jesus Christ according to Matthew): "Joseph and Moses were intimately associated with the court of the Royal Adepts." Then she says — "Solomon sending to Hiram, King of Tyre, for men and materials . . . building of the Temple . . . the famous Tyrian Mysteries must have profoundly influenced the Hebrew esotericism (!!)" ". . . we read of Daniel being educated in the palaces of Babylon, we know that the wisdom of the Magi must have been accessible to Hebrew Illuminati." (Page 3, paragraph ten, *The Mystical Qabalah*. This is one of the books on the list at the end of this book that has some value as an Occult Book for Occult students.)

And this is about the extent of the "history" Dion Fortune gives of the Caballa, leaving us to make what we can out of it.

We can, however, do a little thinking on our own, or rather, a little deducing. Note how she refers to Tyre, then she refers to Babylon and the Magi, and also the word "Illuminati" appears.

All these references imply to me that these ancient religions had, to put it in modern colloquial terms, an "upper crust" in each of their religious systems. An upper crust to which only a privileged layer of someones could gain admittance, or were admitted only by some method of selection.

The logical conclusion to this seeming fact is that everywhere and perhaps everywhen, there was a group of illuminated men and women who had some grip on some "higher" Knowledge which they were using in various ways, "advanced" ways.

Does mundane history show any evidence of the existence of these inner groups? Perhaps if I were a historian, I might know where to look, but the average historian would not know what to look for, exactly. Historians, and others, have mentioned the Eleusinian Mysteries, religious mysteries celebrated at ancient Eleusis in worship of Demeter and Persephone. But little else has been said about these Mysteries. What effect did the rites have on their participants? Were the initiated any "different" after they went through the ceremonies? Were they "better"? If "better," in what ways? character-wise or financial-wise, or both? Or what?

All these questions remain unanswered by the historians. Beyond mentioning how many centuries the Eleusinian Mysteries lasted and some details of the dates of the meetings, nothing was said, and this is not surprising, as the historians-writers-scholars are not as a rule religiously inclined, let alone Occult religiously inclined enough to even wonder about the subject as we do.

Regarding these Eleusinian Mysteries, you can get a great deal of Knowledge about them from three sources, enough so that as time passes and you become proficient in Occult Knowledge you can reconstruct the Mysteries, perhaps not in exact details, but close enough so that you can understand them and arrive at the same benefits that the ancients obtained.

The three sources I mentioned are: One — all the ordinary history accounts of the Mysteries, their seasonal dates, descriptions of their festivals and parades, etc. Two — the study of the Goddesses involved, who and what they were, what they did, what their functions were, how they operated, careful analysis of all the myths about them and their actions and their relations to mortals — and to you students, especially their positions on the Tree of Life. And third — your Inner perception contacting the Akashic records and "reading" therefrom the Knowledge stored there regarding the Eleusinian Mysteries.

As time passed the Eleusinian Mysteries passed away, due I believe to the growing power of the Christian religion. Probably it went "underground" for a time and then that, too, passed away, but probably the initiated were forewarned by their Personal Powers of the coming events.

I regret very much that I will not be able to give you an exact history of the Caballa, as it just does not exist in an exact form. Dion Fortune says that it was not until the fifteenth century when the overwhelming power of the

Church was weakened that some of the Caballa material appeared written down (*some,* she said).

I am inclined to think that it was when printing was invented, or rather, reinvented in the West after being used, in different forms, in China for many centuries, that the whole magical curriculum, some parts definitely false, began to appear in print, because of a good market for it.

Also, I now recall that a large amount of magical material seemed to be in existence even before then. I recall that one of the Popes gave Charlemagne a magical book of daily prayers, the seven mysterious Orisons. Here it is for your use. Use it and see if it gets any results for you! Can't hurt you.

(The next several paragraphs are reproduced from a book by Arthur Edward Waite, entitled *The Book of Black Magic and of Pacts,* published in London in 1898. The book has since been reprinted in paperback form, and the material in it is well known from different sources. It really contains no Black Magic or any Pacts, but probably should be owned by you for research purposes.)

God, by whom all the faithful are saved, give unto me Thy peace, to remain with me for ever, both in this Life and that which is to come. Amen.

MONDAY

O great God, by whom all things have been set free, deliver me also from all evil. O great God, who hast granted Thy consolation unto all beings, grant it also unto me. O great God, who hast succoured and assisted all things, aid me also, and succour me in all my necessities and miseries, my enterprises and dangers; deliver me from all the hindrances and snares of my enemies, both visible and invisible, in the Name of the Father who created the whole world, in the Name of the Son who hath redeemed it, in the name of the Holy Ghost who hath accomplished the entire law in its perfection. I cast myself utterly into Thine arms, and place myself unreservedly under thy holy protection. Amen. May the blessing of God the Father Almighty, of the Son, and of the Holy Ghost, be always with me, Amen. May the blessing of God the Father, who by His only Word hath made all things, be with me for ever, Amen. May the blessing of our Lord Jesus Christ, Son of the great living God, be with me for ever, Amen. May the blessing and Seven Gifts of the Holy Ghost be with me for ever, Amen. May the blessing of the Virgin Mary, and of her Son, be with me for ever, Amen.

TUESDAY

May the blessing and consecration of the bread and of the wine, which our Lord Jesus Christ made when He gave them to His disciples and said unto them: Take and eat ye all of this, for this is My body which shall be delivered for you, in remembrance of Me and for the remission of all sins, be with me forever. May the blessing of the Holy Angels, Archangels, Virtues, Powers, Thrones, Dominations, Cherubim and Seraphim, be with me for ever. Amen. May the blessing of the patriarchs and prophets, apostles, martyrs, confessors, virgins, and of all the saints of God, be with me for ever, Amen. May the blessing of all the heavens of God be with me for ever, Amen. May the majesty of God Omnipotent sustain and protect me; may His eternal goodness lead me; may His boundless charity inflame me; may His supreme divinity direct me; may the power of the Father preserve me; may the wisdom of the Son enliven me; may the virtues of the Holy Ghost stand always between me and my enemies, both visible and invisible. Power of the Father, strengthen me; wisdom of the Son, enlighten me; consolation of the Holy Ghost, comfort me. The Father is peace, the Son is Life, the Holy Ghost is the consoling and saving remedy, Amen. May the divinity of God bless me, Amen. May his piety warm me; may His love preserve me. O Jesus Christ, Son of the living God, have pity upon me a poor sinner.

WEDNESDAY

O Emmanuel, defend me against the malignant enemy, and against all my enemies, visible and invisible, and deliver me from all evil. Jesus Christ the King hath come in peace, God made man, who hath suffered patiently for us. May Jesus Christ, the gentle King, stand always for my defence between me and my enemies, Amen. Jesus Christ triumphs, Jesus Christ reigns, Jesus Christ commands. May Jesus Christ deliver me from all evils for ever, Amen. May Jesus Christ vouchsafe me grace to triumph over all my adversaries, Amen. Behold the cross of our Lord Jesus Christ. Fly, therefore, O my enemies, at the sight thereof; the Lion of the Tribe of Juda and of the Race of David hath conquered. Alleluia, Alleluia, Alleluia. Saviour of the world, save and succour me, I conjure Thee, my God. O Agios, O Theos, Agios, Ischyros, Agios, Athanatos, Elieson, Himas, Holy God, Strong God, Merciful and Immortal God, have pity upon me Thy creature, N. Sustain me, O Lord; forsake me not, reject not my prayers, O Thou, the God of my salvation. Do Thou assist me always, O God of my Salvation.

THURSDAY

Enlighten mine eyes with true light, that they may never be closed in eternal sleep, lest mine enemy should say: I have prevailed over him. So long as the Lord is with me I will not fear the malice of my enemies. O most sweet Jesus, preserve me, aid me, save me; at the name of Jesus let every knee bow, in heaven, on earth, and in hell, and let every tongue confess openly that Jesus Christ is in the glory of His Father, Amen. I know beyond doubt that in what day soever I shall call upon the Lord, in the same hour shall I be saved. O most sweet Lord Jesus Christ, Son of the great living God, thou hast performed most mighty miracles by the sole power of Thy most precious Name, and hast enriched the poor most abundantly, so that by force thereof the demons flee away, the blind see, the deaf hear, the lame walk erect, the dumb speak, the lepers are cleansed, the sick cured, the dead raised up, for wheresoever the most sweet Name of Jesus is pronounced, the ear is ravished and the mouth is filled with pleasant savour; at that one utterance, I repeat, the demons take flight, every knee is bent, all temptations, even the worst, are scattered, all infirmities are healed, all disputes and conflicts between the world, the flesh, and the devil are ended, and the soul is filled with every heavenly delight; for whosoever invoketh or shall invoke this holy Name of God is and shall be saved, this holy Name pronounced by the angel even before His conception in the womb of the Holy Virgin.

FRIDAY

O sacred Name, Name which strengthens the heart of man, Name of life, of salvation, of joy, previous Name, resplendent, glorious, agreeable Name, which fortifies the sinner, Name which saves, conserves, leads, and rules all. May it please Thee, therefore, most precious Jesus, by the power of this same (Name of) Jesus, to drive away the demon from me; enlighten me, O Lord, for I am blind; remove my deafness; set me upright, who am lame, give me speech, who am dumb, cleanse my leprosy, restore me to health, who am sick. Raise me up, for I am dead; give me life once more, and enrich me in all my parts, within and without, so that, furnished and fortified by Thy holy Name, I may abide always in Thee, praising and honouring Thee, because all is due to Thee, and Thou only art worthy to be glorified, the Lord and eternal Son of God, in whom all things rejoice, and by whom all are governed.

Praise, honour, and glory, be given Thee for ever and ever, Amen. May Jesus be always in my heart and in my breast, Amen. May our Lord Jesus Christ be ever within me, may He establish me for ever, may He be around me and preserve me; may He be before me and lead me; may He be behind me and guard me; may He be above me and bless me; may He be within me and give me life; may He be near me and rule me; may He be beneath me and fortify me; may He be always with me and deliver me from all the pains of eternal death, who liveth and reigneth for ever and ever, Amen.

SATURDAY

Jesus, Son of Mary, salvation of the world, may the Lord look favourably upon me, with mildness and propitiation; may He give me a holy and willing spirit, to respect and honour Him only, who is the Liberator of the world. On Him could no one lay hand, for His hour was not yet come, He who is, who was, who shall remain, God and man, the beginning and the end. May this prayer which I offer unto Him deliver me eternally from my enemies, Amen. Jesus of Nazareth, King of the Jews, honourable title, Son of the Virgin Mary, have pity upon me, a poor sinner, and lead me, according to Thy loving-kindness, in the way of eternal salvation, Amen. Now Jesus, knowing what things must come to pass concerning Him, came forward and said unto them: Whom seek ye? They answered Him: Jesus of Nazareth. But Jesus said unto them: I am He. And Judas, who was to deliver Him, was with them. As soon then as He had said unto them: I am He, they fell backward upon the earth. Then asked He them again: Whom seek ye? And they said: Jesus of Nazareth. Jesus answered: I have told you that I am He; if therefore ye seek Me, let these go their way (speaking of His disciples). The lance, the nails, the cross, the thorns, the death which I have endured, prove that I have effaced and expiated the crimes of the unfortunate. Preserve me, O Lord Jesus Christ, from all afflictions of poverty and from the snares of my enemies. May the five wounds of our Lord be unto me an everlasting remedy. Jesus is the Way, Jesus is the Life, Jesus is the Truth, Jesus has suffered, Jesus has been crucified, Jesus, Son of the living God, have pity on me. Now, Jesus, passing went through the midst of them, and no one could place his murderous hand upon Jesus, because His hour was not yet come.

SUNDAY

Pater Noster, & c. Deliver me, O Lord, I beseech Thee, me even, thy creature, N., from all evils past, present, and to come, whether of body or soul; grant me peace and health in Thy goodness; incline favourably unto me Thy creature, by the intercession of the Blessed Virgin Mary and of Thy holy apostles, Peter, Paul, Andrew, and of all the saints. Vouchsafe peace unto Thy creature, and health during all my life, so that, strengthened by the mainstay of Thy mercy, I may never be the slave of sin, nor go in fear of any trouble, through the same Jesus Christ Thy Son, our Saviour, who, being truly God, liveth and reigneth in the unity of the Holy Spirit for ever and ever, Amen. May the peace of the Lord be always with me, Amen. May that peace, O Lord, which Thou didst leave to Thy disciples abide ever with power in my heart, standing always between me and my enemies, both visible and invisible, Amen. May the peace of the Lord, His countenance, His body, His blood, assist, console, and protect me, Thy creature, N., in my soul and my body, Amen. Lamb of God, who didst deign to be born of the Virgin Mary, who didst cleanse the world from its sins upon the Cross, have pity on my soul and my body. O Christ, Lamb of God, immolated for the salvation of the world, have pity on my soul and my body. Lamb of God, by whom all the faithful are saved.

18

This, of course, was long before printing was rediscovered. Also some of this church magic had a suspicious connection to Tree of Life setups. Then again there were some documents dealing with calling, or invoking, certain types of inner plane entities which were connected to various levels of the Tree of Life. This "calling" could not be done without some background knowledge of what and where the entities were located and from which they could be called or invoked.

I would say myself, without making any great research, that from some other hints and scraps of evidence given in this same book, and only because I am looking for it because of the past occult experience I had in accumulating the material for my books, that a great deal of occult Magic was carried on by members of the clergy in the Catholic Church and thoroughly disguised under Church routines.

The following material is also from the same book by Arthur Edward Waite. It is another Catholic Church document which is interesting to our inquiry and, it is entitled *Honorii Papae adversus tenebrarum Principem et ejus Angelos Conjurationes ex originale Romae servato*, Rome 1529. Because of its extreme rarity — few public libraries, *none* apparently in England, possess an example — the authenticity of this work is questioned, and it is impossible to speak with certainty about it. But it is evidently the formularies of exorcism, a rite of the Church, and possesses a considerable body of literature, to which even a Pope of past ages might not inconceivably have contributed. However this may be, the attribution in the one case will account for it in the other. The Grimoire as presented in *The Book of Black Magic* may be merely a perversion of the orthodox conjurations, and if not that, is a reprisal; it is Sorcery revenging herself on a Pope who casts out devils by representing him as the prince of those who dealt with them.

Having said something to justify the Grimoire from groundless condemnation, it is necessary now to add, on the authority of its own evidence, that it is a malicious and clever imposture, which was undeniably calculated to deceive ignorant persons of its period who may have been magically inclined, more especially ignorant priests, since it pretends to convey the express sanction of the Apostolical Seat for the operations of Infernal Magic and Necromancy. The entire claim is set forth most curiously at the beginning of the pseudo-constitution, and must be cited at considerable length to convey its full force:

> The Holy Apostolic Chair, unto which the keys of the Kingdom of Heaven were given by those words which Christ Jesus addressed to St. Peter: I give unto thee the Keys of the Kingdom of Heaven and unto thee alone the power of commanding the Prince of Darkness and his angels, who, as slaves of their Master, do owe him honour, glory, and obedience, by those other words of Jesus Christ: Thou shalt worship the Lord thy God, and Him only shalt thou serve — he hence by the power of these Keys the Head of the Church has been made the Lord of Hell. But seeing that until this present the Sovereign Pontiffs have alone possessed the power of using invocations and commanding Spirits, His Holiness Honorius the Third, being moved by his pastoral care, has benignly desired to communicate the methods and faculty of invoking and controlling Spirits to his venerable Brethren in Jesus Christ, adding the Conjurations which must be used in such case, the whole being contained in the Bull which here follows.
> ## HONORIUS,
> Servant of the Servants of God, unto all and each of our venerable Brethren of the Holy Roman Church, Cardinals, Archbishops, Bishops, Abbots; Unto all and each of our sons in Jesus Christ, Priests, Deacons, Subdeacons, Acolytes, Exorcists, Cantors, Pastors, Clerks both Secular and Regular, Health and Apostolic Benediction. In those days when the Son of God, Saviour of the World, generated in the fulness of time, and born, according to the flesh, of the Race of David,

did live on this earth, whose Most Holy Name is Jesus, before which the heavens, earth and hell do bend the knee; we have seen with what power He commanded demons, which power was also transmitted to St. Peter by that utterance: Upon this rock I will build my Church, and the Gates of Hell shall not prevail against it. These words were addressed to St. Peter as the Head and Foundation of the Church. We then, who, by the mercy of God, and despite the poverty of our merit, have succeeded to the Sovereign Apostolate, and, as lawful successor of St. Peter, have the Keys of the Kingdom of Heaven committed to our hands, desiring to communicate the power of invoking and commanding Spirits, which hath been reserved unto us alone, and our possessors did alone enjoy; wishing, I repeat, by Divine inspiration, to share it with our venerable Brethren and dear sons in Jesus Christ, and fearing lest in the exorcism of the possessed, they might otherwise be appalled at the frightful figures of those rebellious angels who in sin were cast into the abyss, lest also they should be insufficiently learned in those things which must be performed and observed, and that those who have been redeemed by the blood of Jesus Christ may not be tormented by any witchcraft or possessed by the demon, we have included in this Bull the manner of their invocation, which same must be observed inviolably. And because it is meet that the ministers of the Altar should have authority over the rebellious Spirits, we hereby depute unto them all powers which we possess, in virtue of the Holy Apostolic Chair, and we require them by our Apostolic authority to observe what follows inviolably, lest by some negligence unworthy of their character they should draw down on themselves the wrath of the Most High.

Next is Alchemy and the Alchemists' search for the Philosophers' Stone which changes everything into Gold.

The search for the Philosophers' Stone was not hindered by the church, as no matter how fanatic the sweet loving Christ-like Church was in burning heretics they would have to be clear out of their minds to stop any search for Gold, free Gold, which they loved and craved as much as any one did.

I am not making a very good division of dates here, but I trust I am covering the subject in a way that will be informative to you as an occult student rather than as a history student.

There is a direct connection between the Philosophers' Stone and the Tree of Life, which I have written about several times in other places (you'll find the list at the end of the book) and while some persons did find the Stone they didn't mention the Tree of Life as such in connection with the Stone, but the two had to go together, as you will learn in your studies. We always find the Caballa in the background somewhere.

Another historic happening which has strange undertones and overtones to those who are sensitive to Inner Plane pressures, and their following later manifestations out onto the physical plane, is the case of the Knights Templars.

Through their contacts with the nearby Oriental countries they accumulated a high degree of Occult Knowledge and Power, and through the centuries this Occult Knowledge and Power enabled them to acquire great wealth, and as the Order never died this wealth grew somewhat the same as the Roman Catholic Church's wealth does today.°

Some of their Mystic Occult rites were passed on to and became embodied in the structure of the Masons or Masonic Order, although I do admit there is a time gap here which I

° I have since writing the previous material ran across some scraps of historic rumors that the Knights Templars "upper crusts," as stated before, did indeed make contacts with the "upper crusts" of Islam!!! and the two "uppers" found they did have much in common, not only in ordinary things but in the higher revelations of religions!!! So the two "uppers" didn't fight each other but let the lowers do the fighting. I do not know more — see what you can find out.

cannot account for unless I do some intensive research which is not the purpose of this book. I believe the Masonic Order claims their Order goes back to the building of Solomon's first temple or perhaps to Egypt and the building of the pyramids. Or then it could be the other way around, the Knights Templars could have been the outgrowth of the original Masonic bodies' Occult attainment.

At any rate, the Knights Templars were accused of some very peculiar practices in an excuse to seize their vast wealth, which was done. Jacques de Molay, as he was burned at the stake, cursed both the King of France and the then Pope, and they were both dead within the year.

There is a smattering of the Caballa evident in the Masons today, but you can't discuss it with them as they are very cagey and think you are trying to steal their "secrets," especially is this true of new young members. However, like all churches and religions, the mass-bulk of the Masons know very little about their inner structure's secret working nor do they care too much to know. A man named Albert Pike wrote a book called *Morals and Dogma of the Ancient and Accepted Scottish Rite of Freemasonry* which is full of Occult material and some of it that I examined is Caballistic right out. Oh, here is one of their secret symbols I'll expose"! You have seen the Masons' symbol of a compass and a square thusly all the time:

If you ask them what it means, they won't tell because it is a big secret. *Here is the secret:* just connect the open parts on up, and you have two triangles:

Whee! big secret! a fire triangle and a water triangle.

Let us go a little further with this big "secret." Let us take the compass. What does the compass do in real life, working with material things? The compass draws circles, thus delineates and encloses a designated area, puts a specific area inside a boundary. The result is a circle enclosing a space. A circle is a symbol of Air which means movement or ability to move, in this case move in the newly circled enclosed space.

By running an imaginary line across the bottoms of the compass symbol you change the symbol from one kind of a symbol

to another kind of symbol

— a triangle, which in this case is an air triangle and in this case means the same as a circle, and so the symbolism holds together so far.

Now then, consider the other figure of the symbol, the square. What does a square, on the earth physical plane, do? It trues things up according to a plan; remember we are here dealing with Masons whose form of Occult symbolism pertains to building spiritual buildings, after a manner of speaking.

So enough for this — to proceed. We then have two triangles, an upward pointing one and a downward pointing one, thus:

24

These two triangles change into the other two elemental Forces by a line being drawn across the triangle like this:

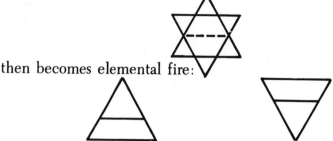

then becomes elemental fire:

then becomes elemental earth. Fire — expansion and Water — contraction — are the two most violent acting elements — alone. Put together they neutralize each other's violent actions and result in solid, inert, placed Elemental Earth. This then, in brief, and in haste, is the meaning of one Masonic symbol.

I have strayed from the history of the Caballa, but it seemed important for me to do so at this point to show some connection between the Caballa and Masonry, this unsuspected, unknown connection, as it were. I can say here that the Caballa system is behind ALL PHYSICAL THINGS. Rules all Physical Things. If you learn to run it, you can "rule" it instead of being at the mercy of unknown and uncontrolled blind Forces. (It could be said that when you *know* you can, then give "eyes" to "blind" forces.)

Now I repeat that I have a strong feeling, based on logic alone, that there exists somewhere a body of men and women who *know*. They have not contacted me probably because I am unworthy (?!). I am not going to make any effort to contact them per se. I'm just going along *learning* and then *using*, and I strongly advise you to do the same.

To try to get back to the history of Caballa thought. Far to the North of Europe lived the Norsemen, or the Vikings — those who lived in the coast indentations called Vicks. These men rapidly outgrew their available food land and for many centuries raided and invaded the countries south of them.

Their religion was a modification of the Caballa, but a religion in which the worst (to us it seems) qualities of the Gods on the Tree were brought out. (There is nothing to prevent this, the namby-pamby Christian religion notwithstanding — you are a free agent.) (I hear you ask But! do you get punished if you do? I don't know, perhaps the answer lies in reincarnation for adjustments. If the answer is not there, then things *are* in a mess!)

I guess this is a good place as any to line up the Gods a la Crowley's style in *777:*

Symbol	Greek	Roman	Norse	Egypt	Weekday
♅	Uranus	Uranus		Ptah	
♄	Saturn	Saturn-Vertu	Saturn	Isis	Saturday
♃	Zeus	Jupiter	Thor	Amman	Thursday
♂	Aries	Mars	Tevi	Sheskit	Tuesday
☉	Apollo	Apollo	Balder (sun)	Ra	Sunday
♀	Aphrodite	Venus	Frigga	Nephtys	Friday
☿	Hermes	Mercury	Loki (fire)	Thoth-Anubis	Wednesday
☽	Diana	Diana		Hathor	Monday
elemental	Pan	Fairies	Trolls		Undines

27

You can see from these diagrams the basic connections of the Gods with the Tree.

The Gods usually perform approximately the same function in all times and places, except as I said, where a God rules several things. The local situation may be such that emphasis upon one feature, not necessarily considered desirable by everybody everywhere, is necessary for survival. This is shown in the case of the Norsemen who outgrew their food supply, and it was either go out elsewhere or stay around and starve. That is, invoke the violent aspects of their Gods.

As a rule, large numbers of new people, strangers with empty stomachs, are not received with open arms in new countries and so it was necessary for these Norsemen to fight terrible battles to escape from their old places to the new and, as I said, to invoke those qualities in their Gods to help them to do this. And thus it is with all peoples with these same Gods — the people use what qualities of their Gods *they need,* and the other unneeded qualities are left unneeded and ignored, so much so that it is even forgotten that they exist in the Gods.

In tracing some evidence of the Caballa system in the history of the Northern Mysteries of the Druids, Celtic, etc., if you are in doubt about the identity of a named God whom you do not recognize, then find out all you can about his or her functions, what he or she does, what stories are told about the God-Goddess.

From a study of these myth stories you should easily recognize the ruling function of the Force in question and place it on the Tree. Once this is done you then know 95% about the God Force and how to deal with it accordingly.

As we are dealing with history of the Caballa in this chapter (although we seem to stray from time to time) I will mention here that there is being published a sort of magazine called MAN, MYTH & MAGIC. At first I received the magazine with some reservation as to its supreme value in our work, but now I have concluded that there is a great deal of valuable historical material being presented, albeit somewhat incomplete due to lack of space. However, at the end of each article further references are given, and all things considered you probably should try to keep the complete file for reference for your Occult study research work.

For example, and this is in line with the historical Caballa chapter we are studying, I noted an article in this magazine about the Norse Gods and especially about the antics of one of their gods, who was called Loki.

This Loki was (or should I say *is*?) a mischief-troublemaker who was always playing around, pulling some kind of trick, often deadly tricks, upon the other Gods. He made endless trouble and was continually being forced, by the head God, to correct the trouble he caused. I wish you would read more about him and then see if, according to his nature, you can recognize him, let us say, among the Greek Parthenon of Gods. (Remember what I said about different peoples with different requirements from the same God.)

In the Occult much balderdash has been written about the Will, and Will Power, almost as if the Will was some kind of a separate power itself instead of being merely an adjutant to a man; a means of steering a man's thoughts in a definite direction and holding them there hard.

Primitive, Stone Age man was very close to Nature as his whole existence depended upon his will power being focused on his surroundings. You become what you think, or rather, you become attached to, merge with, what you think. Those Cro-Magnon men thought so much about the animals they hunted that they merged with the animal's life area and influenced the animals so they were more easily hunted! The somewhat proof of this is that we are here today! Their hunts must have been successful!

These Stone Age men also used "visual aids" for themselves and probably to train the young of the tribe in the magic methods. They drew pictures of the food animals on the sides of their caves and even in some cases of successful hunts.

The man we are discussing is called the Cro-Magnon

man. His remains have been found in a cave at Dardagne, France, along with cave wall pictures, which pictures have a direct connection with the Tree of Life Caballa even at this early human date!!! (See directions at the end of each of my books for making and using a Treasure Chart or Treasure Map, or shall I give it another name? Some name like Life Desire Attainment Outline Chart? I am told that students-people today are not interested in physical supply but only in illumination type of attainment. This can be acquired by means of the Chart, too. By all means make and use a chart — make a chart anyhow, it works while you sleep! If it worked for your Cro-Magnon ancestors, I repeat, it will work for you!)

Next, as we come down the ages, we encounter the organized remains of these Nature contacts embodied in the Celtics and Druids and still later, after the Christian religion had destroyed or driven out the Celts and Druids, what remained was known as Witchcraft, practiced by Witches and Warlocks.

I have reason to believe that the poor old crones who got themselves tortured and burned alive by the sweet Christ-imitating Christians in these screwed-up ages were never the real Witches at all. The lying Roman Catholic Church had spread all manner of lies about Witchcraft in order to thoroughly discredit it, describing the Witches as hideous in appearance and practicing repulsive rites (as witness the descriptions Shakespeare gives of the Witches in *MacBeth* as having beards!). Whereas the opposite is more likely to have been true.

I would guess that the Nature Cult with its nature-natural contacts had gone underground at the first hostile Christian action. The hypocritical Christian cult, by the time it reached those northern countries, England and Normandy, had brought with it something more powerful than Jesus persuasion. The Viking-Norseman might conquer a land, but he soon found that occupying a land, and then settling down and enjoying the land, and acquiring all kinds of goodies by selling his produce and buying what imported products there were available, entailed some quiet arrangements and peace deal-making with his neighbors, instead of killing them as formerly. But all these trading advantages could be gained by preliminary baptism, "prime signing" to the new Christian religion — followed by a later joining to the new religion.

So, as the old nature religion had nothing like this to offer, it went out of sight but was still practiced by many people, for its recognized "spiritual" benefits; and practiced not only by the lower classes but by the "higher classes" also, and probably, I strongly suspect, even had devoted followers *inside* the Church hierarchy, clear up to the very top!! and I mean top-top.

Thus, to somewhat sum up this history section without going too deeply into basic research, *there exists* "OUT THERE" out on the outer planes a "living" pattern of Forces. These Forces can be called Gods. These Forces can be personified as person-like characters and then called, I repeat, Gods. The personification, giving them names and designated appearances, gives *us* a "handle" to get *to them* to grasp a connection to and with them, to *use* them for our benefit.

Man, you and I, Mankind, instinctively *knows* of the existence of these Gods — Forces, concepts — but in our primitive beginning we had no philosophy to attach these concepts to and consequently we acted — worshipped — reacted, blindly — instinctively — intuitively like the Cro-Magnon did with his instinctive Sympathetic Magic cave wall paintings, which sympathetic magic worked (all that is really important), and will work today.

Later, as time passed and Man became more organized, called civilized, these basic God-knowing instincts became organized into definite patterns, and the history pattern we are now studying and deeply concerned with, is the pattern called the Caballa Tree of Life.

(I realize that in these few lines we have covered an immense gap of time between Caveman, Stone Age man, and the beginning of organized civilizations — a civilization is started, I am told, when a people start keeping a written record of themselves.)

You must realize that in this time gap all degrees of Gods and Inner Plane developments took place. First I would say that man came in contact with the simpler basic Nature contacts (the word Nature comes from the same root source as Mother). These simpler Nature contacts were attracted, and controlled, and used, through the vital living force which is naturally in living blood, and hence the early contacts were not so nice from our viewpoint today, to say the least; even the early Judeo-Christian Bible records "sacrifices" of sheep and doves and oxen, which seem to have passed away at some unknown time-date.

Later the Greek and Roman temples were still offering animals as sacrifices, but I gathered the sacrifice was more or less a part gift offering to the personnel in the Temple, who ate portions of the sacrifice as their due for their services.

Still later on Incense took the place of blood sacrifices to a very large extent as the higher patterns of the Caballa Tree of Life took over.

As history moved along through more time-ages, many endless different named God Forces developed. God Forces with different names, but all the same basic God.

However, in the matter of the Jewish Caballa system, their adoption of the Tree of Life system was a bit different from the previous religious systems, and those systems following, in that the Jews did have a *one only God*, and hence when they set up a Tree of Life pattern, in place of a different God showing up on each Sephiroth, such as with a Greek God system I use, they had, on each Sephiroth, *a different name of the same God.* Viz:

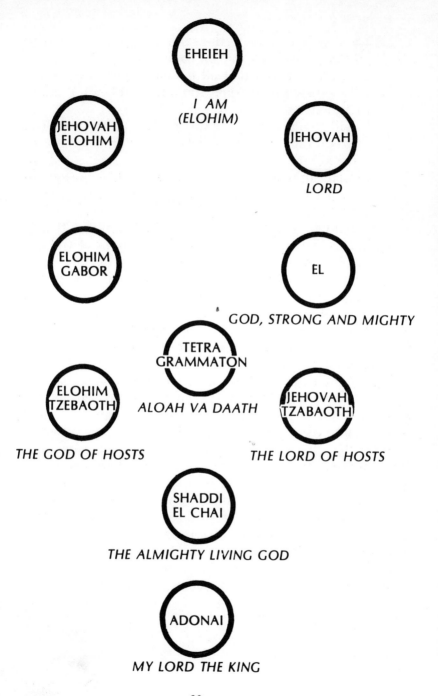

EHEIEH

I AM
(ELOHIM)

JEHOVAH
ELOHIM

JEHOVAH

LORD

ELOHIM
GABOR

EL

GOD, STRONG AND MIGHTY

TETRA
GRAMMATON

ELOHIM
TZEBAOTH

ALOAH VA DAATH

JEHOVAH
TZABAOTH

THE GOD OF HOSTS

THE LORD OF HOSTS

SHADDI
EL CHAI

THE ALMIGHTY LIVING GOD

ADONAI

MY LORD THE KING

This idea is essentially the same difference as it is to have a different God appear on each Sephiroth.

It is a basic truism that all is *One*. Everything is one thing. All Gods are really one God only manifesting under different functions.

We will go no further into this subject at this point, but I plan to continue it out in detail in later chapters, or another book.

A simple summary of the history of the Caballa system (Caballa is a sort of old Jewish word meaning to receive) down to today.

It would appear, from closer study and research than is given in this little chapter, that the foundations of Caballa Knowledge go back into the dim beginnings of the human race, long before there was a language to express the Knowledge.

Apparently, "Mother"° Nature was always there with instinctive, intuitive access to Her secrets, which secrets were perceived then, and are still to be perceived now, by uniting oneself with Her.

This sounds impossible, or at least mysterious, but it is not. It is gratifyingly amazing how Mother Nature will reveal Herself to you upon your observing Her works and entering into communication with Her; to be more exact — to enter the aura of Her operations — once you have done this you are in tune, or receiving good vibrations from Her, and, while the exact process is unknown to me, She gives Her secrets freely to Her, shall we say, friends?

One example I know of — (except I have no dates at hand, but they can be easily ascertained) — there was an old wise woman in England, who had a reputation as a local good Witch, who had a medicine for dropsy and similar sicknesses in which the body tissues accumulated water. A

° Let us use this word Mother Nature for a while. Mother Nature is Isis, the Great Mother of all People and things. She is attached to the Sephirah Binah and is a female Saturn, or the female or negative side of Saturn. Saturn is the positive side. Get used to this idea of different Gods and Goddesses being attached to the same place on the Tree.

big shot Bishop was dying of this accumulated water in the tissues, and after the doctors of his day had given him up, his housekeeper slipped him a slug of the Witches brew. And his heart strengthened and pumped the water from his tissues into the kidneys, from whence it was eliminated, and he recovered!

Of course this recovery attracted the attention of the doctors. They bought the medicine's recipe from the old woman, and found the medicine was composed of twenty-five herbs. Upon testing, it was found that the herb that did the work was Foxglove or the extract drug digitalis, which is still used for this purpose today.

So the big unanswered question of all this is — how did this old woman discover this quality of this plant? And the answer is — Nature disclosed this "secret" to her by in-tuition° — something in the way of her life put her close to Nature's forces. I would not know how exactly. I would have to go through a contact process myself and so would you — but the process is there for all to use freely.

So thus in the beginning, before the dawn of civiliza-tion Mother Nature, who is the Caballa, was there, and still is.

Then as time comes down to three or four thousand years ago, civilizations began to appear in the form of cities and also the Mother Nature Forces became more organized. Religions and temples and priests appeared, and the Forces are reduced to some kind of a system. However, the system

---

° A woman's body has creative powers as you well know, the power to create and form and build up another life body. This, in spite of all the present bull about the differences in treatment of men and women in life (which I, myself, never did subscribe, too, even way back in my childhood). The differences in treatment of women should never have been brought about, but for some reason unknown, to me, it came about. When a woman becomes of a certain ad-vanced age, her body changes the possible birth creation process, a change call-ed "the change of life." THE LIFE CREATION PROCESS THEN GOES TO ANOTHER PART OF THE WOMAN'S BODY, LET US SAY TO HER HEAD — AND SHE BECOMES CREATIVELY INSTINCTIVE-PSYCHIC. INSTEAD OF PHYSICALLY CREATIVE. And then when she showed some signs of this enhanced psychic ability she got burnt at the stake for being a witch, mostly by the sweet, loving Jesus-following Christians!!!!

was understood, and used, and available only to a group of "insiders," generally a priesthood of a specific kind.

The advance of civilization, for want of a better word, the putting of original Nature Forces into a closed system, had the tendency of separating people from their original life power sources, and brought on the queer neurosis that civilized society has today, as witness the hippies, with their dress and manners, and their drugs. All of which is, if you will examine it closely, an attempt to get back to some kind of an original authentic source (the drugs bring about an immediate state of now-ness, is-ness, am-ness, which is missing from our postponed-to-the-future type of living; even in the prevailing religions all teaching are based on a future, postponed, state of rewards and punishments.)

Then as time moved on, other civilizations arose with a different *named* set of Gods but still the same Gods.

Apparently each successful wave of conquerors attributed their conquering success to the favor of their Gods (but the Gods were basically the same Gods!)

The intuitive Truth seems to be more likely that groups (national groups — incarnated groups!) run in cycles, wherein a defined group will display for a time, and then recede to impotence and be crushed in turn, in time.

Through all this the Caballa system survived, and survived, I strongly suspect through the agency of a "hidden" group of Inner Upper Knowers, whose knowledge and powers transcended all group and national bonds. In point of fact, one of these instances is quite plainly brought out in the Bible in Daniel 1:3.

"And the King spake unto Asphenaz the master of his eunuchs, that he should bring *certain of the children of Israel, and of the King's seed, and of the Princes.*

Verse 4: "Children in whom was no blemish, but well favoured, and skilful in all wisdom, and cunning in knowledge, and understanding science, and such as had ability in them to stand in the king's palace, and whom they might teach the learning and the tongue of the Chaldeans."

So here is a record of a definite transference of conquering power to the conquered. Instead of these Chaldeans concentrating exclusively on training their own children they also select a number of children of the conquered King's seed, and of the princes' (seed) and teach the lore and learning of the Chaldeans, or, as Dion Fortune says, "When we read of Daniel being educated in the palace of Babylon we know that the wisdom of the Magi must have been accessible to Hebrew illuminati." (So you can read between the lines as well as the next one.)

As I said, as we come down through the time ages, we find another system has sprung up in darkest Africa. A System analogous, in many ways, to European Witchcraft, in that this system dealt with and along many of the same lines that Witchcraft did.

The system is called Voodoo. Voodoo is a religion practiced in all of Africa.

I have not made an intensive study of the Voodoo religion system as such, but I do recognize one of their Gods, whom they call Papa Legba, and who is the keeper of the gateway (to and from the land of the dead). If Papa Legba is the guide-controller of the dead, then he is a kin to Anubis, the "lower" form of Thoth-Mercury. There are other Voodoo Gods all with the prefix name Papa — Papa Damballa, Papa Gede, Papa Agasu.

(There is a description of a Voodoo ceremony given in Kenneth Roberts' book LYDIA BAILEY, chapter XV to the end. For your occult education, I would advise you to read the whole chapter.)

Thus in ancient (and modern) Voodoo we find the framework of the Caballa. Indeed everywhere you look on this earth plane you find the framework of the Caballa as the whole Physical World is hung on to IT, or would you prefer to use the word "fastened" to it?

So that is about it — a simple history of the Caballa System, the part that can be used by you; the rest of the history, and God knows how big the Truth really is, can be recovered piece by piece by meditation and contemplation if you should need it.

Preface to Chapter 2

In trying to understand God and the World, or Physical Universe, there are a number of ways to go about doing it.

Generally a story of some kind is told, a story called a fable or myth. Also generally the story is about some kind of super-human being who performs actions, which actions result in certain kinds of results from which an example is derived, which example is supposed to be final and un-arguable.

What I would like to call to your attention here is the fact that a story-myth-fable is often misunderstood, as it filters lower-ward in contact with less mentally alert persons, and becomes considered a REAL STORY HAPPENING instead of a fable and here the trouble starts. The dumbbells, not being able to understand parable or illustrations, and being in the majority, will kill off or, at least, drive out the illuminated ones who accept the things-stories as fables; and the whole matter ends up in a mess — with people still looking on Mount Ararat for parts of an imaginary ARK!!!

However this should not be the situation with you; you should *know* that whatever system is used to teach with/by, the teaching is metaphysical, not physical.

The system Ophiel uses (and tries to use better and better) is the Caballa system, and more exactly the phase of the Caballa system diagram called the "Tree of Life."

The Caballa system will be explained and re-referred to again and again in the pages following, even some repetitions made as we go along. Then, too, I have noticed that I come to a place where there are several subjects to be handled at once, and I will say — I will handle this later on. I have handled most of these points later on, but if I don't, I will do it in another book. This I swear.

The first parts here will be talk-theory, followed by some diagrams. If you are puzzled at first, wait for the diagrams.

Chapter 2

You, The Tree, Your Powers

You are the Caballa Tree of Life! A small one, of course, but all the parts of the Tree are in you, and you are in it.

You, the real you, is not the physical body. I never thought we were the physical body, or that our Life, our being, our thoughts, our feelings were generated by our physical being, but I have a book here in which a wild debate is held in which the two sides are presented. The one side claiming that thought is generated by the body and in the body, and the other side saying that thoughts, and life processes, are merely carried on *through* a body; but the origin of these things lies on *another* plane altogether. I always did feel that this idea was nearer the truth. Man is, basically, a pure Be-ing, a living Be-ing, who has, probably against his will, "clothed" himself in "layers" of "matter" and descended from pure being to a physical body-being-life, for some reason not given out by any God (?) governing the operation. Unless *man* is not a piece of God and did it himself! (for experience?)

Anyhow you are "here" now, and you are here in a certain form-framework, and all the connecting memory links as to why-how are lost-suppressed so you will have to start from this end and recover your powers-being-Knowledge back upwards, so first use your powers here to start back up.

For the understanding of these personal powers, and your place in the Universe, to repeat again, one of the endless systems of explanations called Philosophies is a system called the Caballa (spelled in several different ways, but here the spelling Caballa will be used).

41

This Caballa system has been wrongfully attributed exclusively to ancient time Jewish sources whereas apparently a closer examination shows the Caballa system coming from many ancient religious sources and not exclusively Jewish at all.

The reason why the Caballa seems to have this Jewish origin is that among ancient peoples the Jewish religion was the only religion having a monotheistic foundation idea of One God only, and this One God only idea was necessary in the beginning study of the Caballa system. It is not until one becomes more advanced that broader multiple God concepts can be introduced into the study and use of the Caballa system. °

The next few paragraphs will contain some general information about the Tree of Life diagram you are coming to and some ideas of the colors you are going to use and then some information about the various other "Trees" around.

The Caballa is generally shown as a diagram which is called the Tree of Life, as indeed it is. It is also incidentally the original Christmas tree, which came to us through the AngloSaxon Norse-Christian conversions through England.

The diagram of the Tree of Life should be drawn and painted by you and kept where you look at it continually and contemplate its meaning. As you might have trouble drawing the Tree I will try keeping copies on hand, for a nominal sum, to cover the printing and postage which, God knows what it will go up to in the future. So write to the address given and inquire for today's price, and you'll also get your name on a mailing list for new developments. As a

---

° I have changed my mind a little bit here about this monotheistic Jewish conception being at all necessary. I don't want to advocate any kind of multiple Gods and Goddesses worship as I, myself, don't seem to "worship" anything in particular. I am conscious all the time of the presence of a *"First Cause,"* with which I want to become *more* in contact — is this worship?

The various Gods and Goddesses attached to the various Sephiroth to me mean only Forces, FORCES-VIBRATIONS each with a certain characteristic and practically nothing else. Our growth job here is to understand these characteristics and to cooperate with them — fit in with them — and thus "ride" the Forces.

matter of fact after doing the first Tree of Life in the Queen scale of colors you should do a Tree in the King scale: but by this time you should be making your own diagrams.

Then for me to seemingly make it still more confused — you will find later there are four "layers" to the Tree, and each of these has a colored Tree of its own! For example, on page 139 of Dion Fortune's book *The Mystical Qabalah* in the description of Binah, in the four "layers" the colors are: 1. Crimson (King scale); 2. Black (Queen scale); 3. Dark Brown, and 4. Grey flecked pink. So you should eventually make four more Trees! They have their uses in your future Magic operations. But notice that Dion Fortune mentioned these other trees, but just that, mentions, and that is all she does. Never a hint for you to make the other Tree diagrams because that hint could lead to another hint that there was more there than met the eye, and this would be giving away secrets! Secrets that you're not entitled to KNOW (because somebody considers you unworthy). (I don't.)

To get going — the physical Universe is what the Caballa Tree of Life is concerned with and is what we are concerned with. What went on before the physical universe came into being is nothing that we can handle or do anything about now. Dion Fortune calls them the three negative veils of existence, so let the matter go at that.°

I am not prepared to explain an absolute physical beginning, nor am I really interested in one as such. I don't think any man was around to witness it. There are some people who set up a big cosmogony of rounds and rays like

_____

° Since writing the above I have come onto a whole new mass of material which is to be put out in the next book which I am not hustling you to buy or to neglect this book as this book is a foundation to the next book. To make a long story longer I didn't know, as I said, about the way the "revelations" were going when the above was written. The whole mass of material in my books so far and coming out, as it did, step by step, led around in a large circle to the old Gnostics and their religious concepts, which I had no idea about, but which is now emerging by itself from these books that now I realize wrote themselves. As I said in the next book we will deal with the beginnings of what was known as the Gnosis, and you will find that another whole new world of good ideas should open up for you, ideas that you can use — USE.

Madame Blavatsky in her works, but I find the rounds and rays vastly boring, and of no importance in handling today's problems, other than to feel all will come out in the wash! which it will, but to hell with sitting around and doing nothing to assist yourself in the meanwhile.

So in our study of the Caballa Tree of Life system we will assume a place when the preliminary physical creation pattern has taken place already AND CREATED OUT OF ITS SELF (as there is no other material around — how could one think there is something "there" besides God, some other material or matter existing besides God?). Therefore it seems that the conclusion is inescapable that ALL WAS GOD. ALL IS GOD and ALL WILL BE GOD especially ALL IS GOD. So re-examine all matter with this idea in mind.

So then we can start with a Tree of Life pattern already made up, and this pattern is to be made real and physical.

The undifferentiated God essence substance enters the Tree of Life pattern at Kether and then becomes, in some way unknown by any teacher I know, Physical Elemental Essence Substance.

The Physical Elemental Essence Substance then proceeds on down the Tree, becoming denser each step lower, until it becomes final dense matter (but only seeming!! This seeming will be covered as we go along, I hope!).

At this place we will consider the Paths on the Tree.

You have noted that the Tree of Life consists of ten round circles connected together by double lines running from one circle to another. These double lines are called Paths. The round circles are called Sephiroth, which apparently means to emanate, which of course means to come out of, and these Sephiroth do come "out" of each other. The Sephiroth are objective, and the Paths are subjective.

I know you students are of good intelligence, but these terms ob-jective and sub-jective bothered me especially in connection with Occult studies.

In the Occult, the words Objective and Subjective have

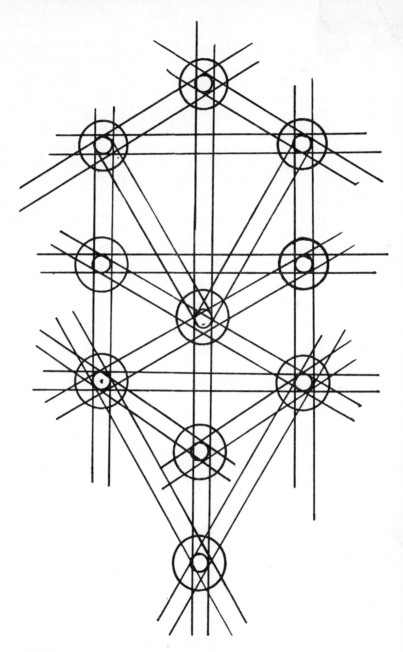

.This figure (Fig. A) is a diagram which will enable you to make up Trees of Life easily. This figure is a good working size. Just take off the measurements with a measuring compass. Then make the circles in pencil as well as the little circles. Following the lines of the little circles make the paths in pencil, too. Then ink in the whole Tree. Carefully. After the ink is dry, then erase the pencil lines remaining with a gum eraser.

specialized meanings. The word objective stands for a physical plane object, while the word subjective stands for the inner plane duplicate of the outer physical plane material objective, clear on "Up" or "In," to the original archetype. The dictionary definitions are different.

This seems like a good place to put in the statement that, as you have no doubt been told already, the Paths and the Sephiroth have been equated to the Tarot Card deck. The Paths are the Major Arcana, and the Sephiroth are the Minor Arcana. There is a discrepancy here as to numbers of Sephiroth and cards in a deck, but it should be explained later.

Each of the Sephiroth has a special characteristic which sets it off as different from the other Sephiroth.

So much so are these Sephiroth different from each other that, in the Jewish montheistic system, each Sephiroth has a different name of the one God.°

These different names of the one God designate the different *functions* that the *same God* performs in that place or position.

The translators of the Bible in many cases translated these various *different* God names into just plain God or

---

° To me this point is so interesting and so vital that I am adding this additional information about it. Basically One is to become the Many. The one vibration is to become the many vibes (to give it a little touch of the mod). Each of these different vibrations acts differently from the other and was designated as a separate, special, God, or Goddess in the form of the Tree of Life that I use the most, using the Greek Pantheon as the basis.

You do understand, don't you, that the elements that constitute this Physical Life ARE DIFFERENT FROM EACH OTHER? This-these differences are personified-dramatized in the form of Gods and Goddesses each carrying on a certain kind of function and "ruling" a certain aspect of Physical Existence.

These differences, however, are only different rates of vibrations of one single main vibration.

Another way of saying this is that there is only one GOD, ONE FIRST CAUSE, and HE-IT functions in different ways the same as the different Gods and Goddesses function, and this different functioning is shown by giving a different GOD NAME to each of the Sephiroth as shown on Tree of Life No. 2. Please study these ideas carefully as they form a large part of the background of the Caballa Knowledge.

Lord, or when they did translate the God name, as El —
God strong and mighty — the significance was lost on the
ordinary Bible reader because he didn't relate the name
"God strong and mighty" to its position on the Tree of Life.

At this point of this study it seems about the right time
to set up a Tree with the Hebrew names for the different
functions of God upon it.

Note the Tree of Life with the following Jewish God
names on the designated Sephiroth.

I will try to explain the meaning of some of these names
to you now. That is, the general accepted ordinary
meanings, that you can and will use in your present Magical
work. Of course there are deeper meanings unto
endlessness, and I, unlike Occult fakers out there, will tell
you "I do not know it all," but neither do they, but catch
them admitting it! In time, after you (and I) learn the first
lessons, we will be ready for more and higher lessons. So
let's go!

The first group of God names we will look at is Jehovah
and Elohim, also Tetragrammaton, and El.

Jehovah is one of the most misunderstood names in the
Bible and Occult setup references.

In the first place Jehovah is not a name. Jehovah is a
formula!!! (The occult ignorants translate Jehovah — Lord.)

Jehovah is spelt Yod, Heh, Vav and Heh, or in Hebrew
from right to left ה ו ה י , and is, as I said, a formula, not
a name.

The formula is shown by the meanings of the letters
composing the formula Jehovah.

The first letter of Jehovah is a Hebrew Yod י . This
letter is the smallest letter in the Jewish alphabet. Also each
letter in the Jewish alphabet has or is a name of a thing, too.
In this case the letter Yod means hand, or a closed hand.
Also the letter Yod stand for I (i), as in I am. I the central
center of consciousness, the central I, the person personality.

Back to the formula. So far we have a Yod, which
means I (I am).

47

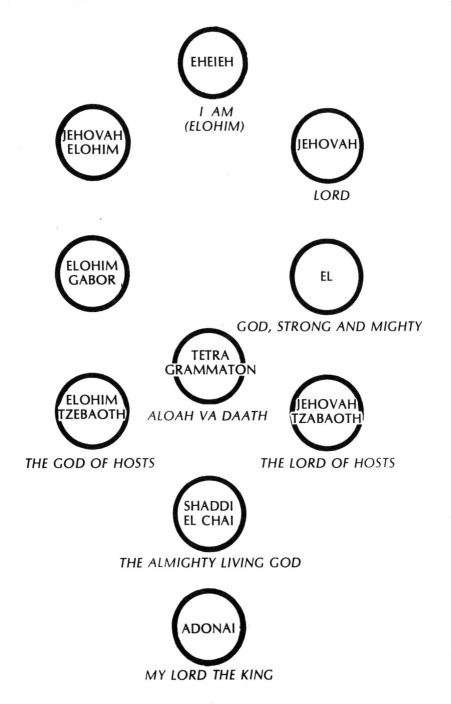

The next letter is Heh ה (h). The meaning of Heh is window or wind-door, an opening through which Air (elemental Air — movability) can enter a house (place). Also through a wind-door can be seen or viewed a scene, or, in the case of a mind, an imagination image picture of something.°

Back to the formula. So far we have a י which is I and a ה wind-door.

The next letter is Vav י . The word Vav means nail, also has a sort of meaning of desire accomplished-finished. A nail fastens two things together. You can also say desire fastens or puts two things together.

And then a final Heh ה with a dot in the middle of it, which dot means this Heh is a solid not an imaginary one.

Here is the whole Lord, Jehovah, formula. What it means is — You see, in your mind's "eye" what you want — want is desire, the nail that fastens your sight, inner sight object, to YOU, you then possess the object in imagination, and later you can possess the object in "real" through a process of Magick transformation, which process is started by the formula.

This then appears to be the meaning of the God name Jehovah, and you note this name Jehovah appears throughout the Tree, especially on the right side of the Tree, as you look at it. Later on this will be treated more fully.

The other Elohim appearing more often on the left side of the Tree, you facing it, is, I am told, a masculine God name El with a feminine name ending (El)ohim. Dion Fortune says this word Elohim means God and Goddess, or male and female God principles in one, somewhat reminding me of Mrs. Mary Baker Eddy's Father-Mother God.

There appears to be a good reason for their appearance

° Dear students — None of these examples are exactly exact — you have to juggle your mind and stretch it slightly to make it "fit" all these ideas — as the "Masters," it seems, didn't want to make the whole thing too clear, they wanted YOU to WORK to UNDERSTAND these things and their applications to LIFE LIVING.

on your left-hand side of the Tree, but this, too, will be handled later.

At one place, Tiphareth, or the Sun, the word Tetragrammaton appears. This is a Greek word that got in here someway, and it means the same as Jehovah; the word Tetragrammaton means the four-lettered word, Jehovah ‏ה ו ה י‎ . Adonai means my lord the/a king.

Next we will consider the Tree of Life labeled Tree Number Two, and the names thereon.

In my opinion these Tree Number Two names have a lot of blinds in them, and conceal rather than reveal the Truth about the Tree of Life.

I have said before in other times and places, that the Occult and Occult-appearance teachings have a lot of blinds and dead ends and outright lies in them.

I am not fully sure what this is for, or why, or how much of this is intentional, and how much is due to just plain ignorance on the part of those who should know better. I am not a blowhard so I am going to say it this way. I am reasonably sure that many of the statements made about the Occult are not correct, and if you study long enough with powerful desire to know Truth, you should get a disquietness, an uneasy feeling that something is not right, when you study some certain Occult subject, and you should get a connection-feeling that a certain statement is not correct — and then the correct idea should come to you, and your mental checks should show it reasonably certain.

Back to Tree of Life Number Two — you will note the "top" or first Sephiroth is labeled Kether, which means Crown.

Dion Fortune's book *The Mystical Qabalah* has been referred to before, and I suggest that you should get the book and read it many times. *The Mystical Qabalah* is the only near understandable book on the Caballa that I have ever found.

I do not know how much of this book Dion Fortune got from her inner contacts and how much she got from original

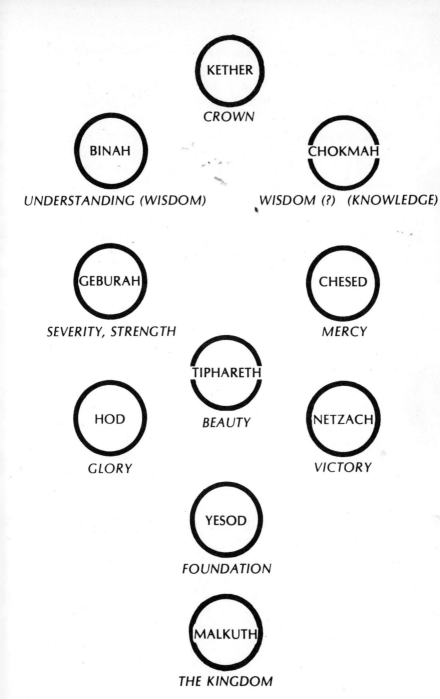

51

research — however we have it, and so let's master it, and then we can go on to whatever is next.

Many of Dion Fortune's statements and data on the Caballa are on a very high level and of no use to us "down here."

Also, there are well-recognized correspondences (she says) to parts of the Tree which I have to strain myself to understand, and accept her statements about these parts.

For the time being, I am merely going to mention some of these differences, but do not let me suggest anything untoward to you. Follow all the lines given and look to your future development to answer your questions exactly.

It won't hurt for you to follow my references to the Tree of Life in this book from now on, if you have the book. You should have it eventually. You can get it from SAMUEL WEISER, INC., 740 Broadway, New York City, NY 10003.

Crown is not too bad a name, in an ordinary sense, as Kether is at the top of the Tree like a top crown, but to a new seeker in the Occult it doesn't mean too much, nor did it mean too much to me when I first saw it, rather confusing to be truthful.

I am of the opinion a rather better word (for me at least) would be "Opener," and, in fact, an Egyptian God, attached to this Sepiroth is Ptah, the "Opener," which is a million times more Occult instructive to me than the name Crown.

In Greek myths of the creation of the world Uranus (Ouranos) is the first God ruler. Read in the myths what happened to him and see what that idea means to you. Also you had better make up a sheet of paper similar to the book sheets and make your own circles for Sephiroth on it with the names I am suggesting to you now, and any other names that *suggest* themselves to you *personally*.

Next we "come down" to Chokmah which name is supposed to mean Wisdom. I have a strong feeling that Chokmah's true name should be Knowledge. Another true name for Chokmah should be Chaos, following the very old

Greek myth name, and the ancient meaning for this word "Chaos" means "Gap" or "space" (to operate in), and space to operate in is certainly the function of Chokmah after the "Opener."

Dion Fortune tells about some very scary beings called the Qliphoth demons which are presumably created by an over-plus surplus of each normal Sephiroth's functions (which sounds kind of silly to me but is probably true). (But don't worry about them, you'll never see one!)

So if you will read the attendant confusion and messes involved in Gayley's story of the myths involving the creations of the world like the coming into existence of the Hecatonchires, the hundred-handed monsters, etc., you can well understand that before physical things could settle down there was bound to be some confusion, and the confusion could well explain the existence of the Qliphoth in another manner.

We now move over to the next Sephirah which is named Binah and which is supposed to mean Understanding, but which, to me, should be named Wisdom instead of Chokmah as aforesaid. However on second thought, Understanding is a type of Wisdom.

Let us go back to Tree of Life chart number one, the one with the God names on it.

Here Binah is labeled Jehovah El-ohim, which is certainly extraordinary to say the least, and Dion Fortune does not say a word about it, nor can I find anything about it elsewhere. °

The actual meaning of this name Jehovah Elohim would seem to be Lord of Lords (ettes), add something to indicate that Lords means feminine Goddesses, too.

° The name Elohim is very mysterious. I am too old to go into this too deeply now as I will never live long enough to get to the scholastic bottom of the matter. I am told, and I have to accept this for now, that the name Elohim is a name of a male God with a female plural Goddess ending. If you will study my book *The Art and Practice of the Occult,* you will find in that book the idea that the Tree of Life is divided into three parts, as you can see, and I have equated those three parts with Future — Present — and Past. Therefore considering the

To repeat, the name Jehovah Elohim would seem to mean that in this Sephirah the ruler also ruled all the governing Forces, objective and subjective, which governed functions-creations on that side of the Tree.

I am aware that none of the above material is similar to what Dion Fortune, and others et al. put out, which you can note by reading her book as I have previously recommended.

She goes off on tangents like Ama the dark sterile Mother, Aima the bright fertile Mother, etc. I would just as soon she had cut out this flowery language and got down to brass tacks. I note that after the First Cause has made his entrance in Kether, He-It — the Father-Mother God of Christian Science — has carved out a working area for itself in Chokmah, the next step is to set up "housekeeping" in Binah. Also note that what goes into "housekeeping," which in a sense can be likened to going to a "form," must sometime come out of the form.

Look at your Tree Number One sheet. Note it was Jehovah who ruled Chokmah. Review that Jehovah was a formula — now in Binah the formula is coming "true." The second Heh is becoming solid, and the solidity starts in Binah and ends up in Malkuth, finally.

I would suggest again that you reread Dion Fortune's description of Binah. She goes off on many a beautifully turned phrase such as "Form is the discipline of Force." Well, sure it is, but while you should read this it really doesn't do you too much good in a practical way, but you should read and learn it anyhow.

Then in another place she says "the embodied spirit sees death on the horizon as soon as its day dawns!" Sure, as

left-hand side of the Tree of Life, as you look at it, as the future it could be thought that two forces, positive and negative, male and female, forces went into the NEW FIRST CREATIONS, and in a sense, the female force is used up in passing through the present to the past, so the past becomes the male lord alone, just an idea of mine. What do *you* think? However, fortunately much of Occult Knowledge will work without these tremendous fine points being completely understood anymore than a person has to be an engineer to drive an automobile.

I said before, what goes into a form must come out, sooner or later. I myself don't look forward to it, but I try to accept it and write as many books as I can so they can be used after I kick the bucket (written in 1973).

I remember one time I was trying to explain this birth-from-death to a non-Occult student woman, and she almost screamed at me to stop talking. I hope you are not affected that way. I cite this as an example of what one is up against when you try to hand out these ideas to the world, so I don't hand them out any more unasked — there are too many asking.

I read and studied the section in Dion Fortune's book about each of the Sephiroth, and I am amazed at the complex detail she goes in to in elucidating these various Sephiroth and the uselessness of it for everyday living.

I have not had access to the sources from which she got her information, but then I am not trying to duplicate her work but to get some workable tools out of the Caballa system that you can use for your well-being NOW by developing your Understanding.° And when you have a mass of Understanding materials on hand, like a well-stocked library of Knowledge-ideas, this then turns to Wisdom which should help you transform your life the way you want it.

For example, I want you to read page 144 of her book, paragraph 12. Note she uses the word "Antinomeanism."

This word threw me, and I had to look it up. Sounds very impressive, does it not? It means a type of belief in which the moral law is of no effect, only Faith. Now this is all very beautiful, and please get it for what it is worth, but I

° Note: Dion Fortune says on page 6 of the *Mystical Qabalah*, "for this reason, although I shall give in these pages the principles of the mystical Qabalah, I do not consider it would be in anybody's interest to give the keys to its practice even if by the terms of the obligation of my own initiation I were not forbidden to do so"!!!!! Can You Imagine such withholding? Well, don't worry about it. You are getting a bunch of working keys in this book. Working keys that will keep you busy for a very long time to come. And when you run out of the keys in this book, you should then have enough to enable you to get your own Keys!!!!

don't see the knowledge of this word or this paragraph adding to your personal Powers to handle this Physical Plane World.

Also dear Dion used a word I cannot even find in my dictionary. On page 139 she uses the word "Kteis." I have a smaller Collegiate dictionary and a large dictionary, but the word is in neither one. Also, and I intend writing to them about this, I can't find any classical myths or references to a Goddess of Sewers and scavengers named Cloaca, at least not in ordinary texts.

Therefore what I should want you to get from Kether, Chokmah and Binah NOW is — (later I will introduce some of my own discoveries which I sincerely hope will add to what Dion Fortune gave you. I am planning on covering the Tree first in the ordinary way and then going back with the additional!):

Kether is the entrance place of the God subtle "material" (in the first form of ethereal influence) into this Physical World. The ethereal subtle God influence changes into physical matter at the bottom of the Tree (this change is through an *agency* which "changes" the apparently subtle ethereal God Force influence coming in from outside the top — Kether) and, as I said, after traveling all the way down the Tree comes to "rest" at the bottom of the Tree as Physical Matter in Malkuth. But the physical matter down there is no more "real" and "solid" than was the original God subtle material in the first place.

I don't know if I will be able to describe the "*Agency*" in this book or not. I am not sure about its reception and use by the wrong persons. If they are really dumb and do not make it work, then no harm can be done. If they should be able to get it to work the wrong way, it could be awkward for me to explain why I gave the vital information out. So I should exchange a letter or two with the student first, to see what is going on, before handing it out. However, I think I'll drop hints here, and if they figure it out themselves, I guess it's OK then.

For example, I was in a social gathering once where

some devil worshippers were attending. They all had pentagrams around their necks with the one point pointing downward, which is, as you know, a sign of disruption. I looked at them and tested their auras, *and felt nothing,* so I knew they did not activate the inverted pentagrams due to dumbness, but if anybody in that group does activate his pentagram and set off the rest, all hell will break loose!

Incidentally, I noticed a long time ago (no offense intended) that the Eastern Star pin seems to have a one point downward pentagram, which I have always wondered about, as it appears to be definitely wrong pointwise, Occultwise.

To get back to the Caballa Tree. As I repeat again. There are endless attributions of all kinds, angels, and archangels, and names and titles, attached to these first three Sephiroth, and of course to the other Sephiroth to come, too.

All these attributions are probably truly true, but many of them you will not use, and if you try to learn them all at once now, it gets confusing. Learn the simple basic facts now, start to use the learned knowledge, and as you get deeper into the Occult and your obvious power-knowledge-wisdom increases, you will then pick up these other different extended Knowledge matters one by one and "go to town" with your Occult work and Occult development.

So far now you can sum up these first three Sephiroth viz — Kether is the place where the First Cause (called the Anglo-Saxon name God which means Good) enters this Physical Plane Universe from "out" there somewhere (Heaven alone knows from WHERE!!) HE-IT — The Father-Mother-Male-Female conjoined principles — first two sides of this one IT thing — (nothing, *but just nothing,* is so thin that it does not have two sides) utters the thought-words Eheieh (I am) (could mean, let us speculate a little, "here" I am, a part physical IT) (so what comes next?): "I will carve out a sphere of action for me to operate-move about in."

Hence, as Dion Fortune says, IT moved — overflowed

— into a space to operate in, which space is called Chokmah. (Again, read about the creation of the world in Gayley's *Classic Myths* — note the names Night and Mist and Fiery Air of Aether — Eros. Also note Void, Mass, and Darkness — broadbosomed Earth and Beautiful Love and so on. Do a little simple meditation on these things and see if you can identify any of them working here today — are any of them present in your character and nature? See if you can make friends with them and come to terms with them. Is it possible?)

Now Kether has been changed to Chokmah and the work of expansion begins —

It is said that Chokmah is not a producing aspect of the physical universe so far thus created: Chokmah is a stimulating influence, analogous to a male fertilizing function. I will say in passing at this point and expect to elaborate more fully later, that all the Sephiroth on the right side, you facing the Tree, are, in my opinion, stimulators due to another factor which, again, will be expounded more fully later (if not in this book, then another book).

Also you might, from now on, always look to find the female, or male, counterpart of any God Force we mention. So look for the female counterparts of Chokmah (you'll find them in Gayley).

Chokmah being the great stimulator and having nothing to stimulate but itself, proceeds on to create Binah who is called The Great Mother as Chokmah is called the Great Father, and you can note that Magical images of these two Sephiroth are: 1. Chokmah, a bearded male figure, and 2. Binah, a mature woman, a matron.

Thus Binah is a necessarily created overflow from Chokmah and the creation of a female phase to be used as a broadening creation woman-type organization to receive the male creative direction as to the further expansion of a million different kinds of FORMS. *Remember that the First Cause creates all things out of himself as there is no other "material" present or available to him* for Creation-supply except "himself" or as we have used the term here,

58

ITSELF. Please consider these two outrageous, to our physical plane, concepts. 1. Here is a power with both sexes (?) in it, androgynous (?), hermaphroditic (?), that separates part of itself from itself, and one part makes, creates Forms out of the other part. Yet they are both the same, originally, and *still are* basically both the same THING (WOW!) (better do some meditation on *this* subject!!) and 2. Thus in view of the above obviously logically true facts, all matter, any large or small piece of matter, physical matter is *GOD*, Somewhat different than what the world thinks, isn't it?

Also another little sideline here, there is the second commandment of the famous Ten Commandments which Jehovah gave to Moses on the mountain, but which he must have already given to the Egyptians a thousand years before, as I am told similar commandments were found a thousand years before Moses.

In this commandment number two, God says not to take a graven image of anything and fall down and worship it. No, I guess I'd better put in the whole thing — Exodus Ch. 20, verse 4: "Thou shalt not make unto thee any graven images, or any likeness of anything that is in heaven above, or that is in the earth beneath, or that is in the water under the earth": 5. "Thou shalt not bow down thyself to them, nor serve them: for I the Lord thy God am a Jealous God, venting the iniquity of the father upon the children unto the third and fourth generation of them that hate me; and shewing mercy unto thousands of them that love me, and keep my commandments."

I cannot see myself worshipping any graven image, but according to the previous logic, which appears to be true, at least relatively true, all physical matter is God. So I can't figure out what all the squawk is about. If you can figure it out, let me know. None of it hangs together at a higher level.

Binah, then, is considered the Cosmic Mother from which all things come or are formed in, by, of. Check out the references to Thrones in The Mystical Qabalah. This Throne idea is very illuminating. Any woman in order to give birth to offspring requires a solid base from which to work. Such a base is usually called a home. A home is usually a house built on a piece of ground. The ground and the house structure is ruled by Saturn who is attached to Binah.

Also attached to Binah is Isis. Isis is a sort of female Saturn. Isis is the Egyptian Mother Goddess from which all things spring. Isis's attachment to Binah is Egyptian and Saturn's attachment is Greek. The Egyptian myths are so much older than the Greek myths that the connecting links that should make Isis the mother-ancestor of the lower Gods are not as clear as in the case of Saturn, which clearly show the relationship between the Gods. The only relationship mentioned is Hathor and Nephthys as sisters of Isis. In reality they are the same Goddesses. Hathor is the same as Artemis and Nephthys is the same as Aphrodite.

Of course we have been speaking here as if these Gods and Goddesses were real, and alive, and personal, *and they are not.* In the later part of this book we will treat them differently and show you how to contact them, and use them! But for now, we'll proceed as we have been doing.

The first three Sephiroth are considered as a sort of unity triangle. I have also set up the next three as a sort of unity triangle, too, rather different from *The Mystical Qabalah's* way, as will be shown later.

The right-side pillar of the Tree, as you look at it, is called the Pillar of Mercy; the middle pillar the Pillar of Mildness; and the left-hand pillar the Pillar of Severity.

I cannot cut these names myself, although *The Mystical Qabalah* makes a great to-do about explaining them. To me the first three Sephiroth seem like the Father principle, the next three the Mother principle, the next three a lower Father, and the last one a lower Mother. By all means read and study *The Mystical Qabalah*, but remember there are blinds and traps in the Occult, and if you can't think your way out, or think of and consider additional ideas, it can be very binding to future expansion progress thinking.

After Binah comes Chesed, and Chesed is called Love.

Again I don't cut the name. Chesed is the sphere of Jupiter, and Greek Zeus and Roman Jupiter don't spell much about Love to me (unless you mention Zeus's love affairs, but I suppose that is not what is meant). Also Dion Fortune says Chesed is the corresponding place of anabolism (the digestion of food), and the next Sephirah across — Geburah — is catabolism, or the tearing down of the food products in tissues, etc. This seems reasonable.

She says that Chesed is the sphere of the formulation of archetypal ideas. I have found that the archetypal ideas were formed and started to be carried out in Chokmah, and Binah, or so it seemed to me who once fancied myself an inventor.

You will note that she talks about some very heavy stuff here. The Logos, etc.

This is all of tremendous importance but is not going to get you a loaf of today's bread, which is what I'm trying to get down to now.

We will go on with the next Sephirah. *The Mystical Qabalah* calls it Geburah — Strength, Severity. We know it better by the Roman name of Mars or the Greek name of Aries. And we call him the God of War, etc. He is also the Norse God Tevi from whom our Tuesday comes.

As usual there are a bunch of other wildly romantic tales, titles and such like connected with this Sephirah, all of which are not too much use to me in carrying on daily activities. What am I supposed to do with the Five-petalled Tudor Rose! (Don't answer!)

I do note here a name Seraphim, Fiery Serpents.

The Serpent occurs again and again in the Occult and generally means Wisdom or something like that in Occult usage.

The ancient Occultist, seeing Forces with clairvoyant vision, saw the non-physical force as a vibration-wave like this:

amplitude

wavelength

and to their more primitive understanding this "wave" appeared as a serpent or snake.

No doubt when Moses (there were several "leaders" all named Moses) raised the brass Serpent on a pole in the Wilderness° it had something secret to do with misdirected forces represented as serpents, "raising" the forces on a pole (the spinal column) cured the people of their afflictions of misused force. Although why the hell they go to all the trouble to tell a story in this veiled manner is beyond me, instead of just coming right out and saying, the people misused their Forces, these natural (sex?) Forces, the Forces that look like snakes to clairvoyant sight, and their leader made a symbol snake of brass, or copper, the metal of Venus, and strung it up on an upright pole to point out that the people should elevate their thoughts (?) to higher points, away from too much lower parts, etc., etc.

Mars also rules Police under Dion Fortune's basic Caballa ideas, and this sounds quite true to correspondence.

Dear students, we all are having a hassle these days with the Police and Police Ideas. No one in their right mind can quarrel with the idea of the police preventing crime or catching criminals which should be the main object of the police, but instead of that we find so much of police work today is taken up in attempting to suppress not criminals but people who are doing personal things that other people don't like themselves, but won't let others do. Such things as nude shows in theaters and bars, etc. If people don't want to see those kinds of entertainments, let them stay away and mind their own damn business. There is plenty of police work to be done in crime without bothering about people's

---

° Here is another one of those "queer" contradictions in the Bible on which all preachers are so silent, which silence amounts to hypocrisy. It was my understanding that Jehovah had given a commandment, the second, in which he forbade the chosen people to "take-make" unto themselves any graven image of anything, etc., etc., and to bow down to it, etc., etc. And now here we have Jehovah himself doing that very same thing that he ordered them not to do, if I can read at all correctly. Or could it be that because the brass snake was cast it was not graven, that is carved out of rock-stone — did that make the difference? I don't get it.

morals and junk like that. Let the Church take care of Morals and the Law take care of Crime.

Yet we have a situation here in this country now where a bunch of deadheads can't enjoy anything in life themselves and don't want anyone else to do so either, so hence they got two recent squares on the Supreme Court now and are trying to steal the liberties we gained under the Warren Court (written in June, 1973).

Another misuse of Police Power occurred in the attempt at Prohibition. I am informed that recent evidence study shows that this monster was put over by native American Bible thumpers who didn't like foreigners and their beer gardens and wine-drinking "wimmen." It seemed foreign "wimmen" drank beer and wine!!

As Occultists you should not be led astray by extraneous subjects and should mentally resist all efforts to sidetrack you from your main Occult work. Encourage the police to catch criminals, but discourage them in acts of suppression.

I am not sure just how Mars forces react with each other, but the police, by their rigid actions, have brought down upon themselves much hatred, and this hatred has resulted in violent actions being taken against them by certain other violent classes of people, who are actually killing the policemen by ambush, which is certainly a Mars action or reaction.

Many of these things appear to be the fault of Politicians and rigid classes of people who cannot make adjustments to allow others their personal freedom choices (much due to Roman Catholic Church pressure, which Church loves to rule and dictate its will upon people.)

Many politicians make silly foolish laws which encourage the oppressed to seek aid from other politicians to evade these silly ill-advised laws. I will write more on this later and connect with the Occult.

Next we come down to the center Sephirah which is called Tipareth, which is supposed to mean Beauty. I'm sorry, but frankly I don't get the beauty at all unless it is in connection with the Greek Apollo who has been called "Glorious Apollo."

Dion Fortune speaks of Mysteries of the Crucifixion with this Sephirah, thus making some kind of a connection with Jesus Christ and other crucified Gods or slain Gods or sacrificed Gods which, as she does not explain further, I am totally unable to follow out in any way.

Please again don't think I am denigrating myself or am totally ignorant. There may be all sorts of secret mysteries here, and I just never, to this date, came across them. I will, however, never cease searching as long as I am alive, and if and when I uncover anything valuable, I'll give it to you quickly.

As I said, this central Sephirah is called "Beauty," and I don't get the beauty at all so I think it is another of those innocuous blinds so prevalent in the Occult.

Tiphareth is on the "Middle Pillar" as Israel Regardie calls this center column in his book.

It does seem, from its position, that Tiphareth is a sort of gathering together and balancing up Force which we will go into further, as I said already several times.

Dion Fortune speaks of this sphere being connected with the Knowledge and Conversation of our Holy Guardian Angel but doesn't say much about how to contact it in a practical way, evidently leaving it to some kind of a gradual growth idea which I myself find very unsatisfactory. But read her high-sounding language and see what you get out of it. (A practical quick connection would be wonderful.)

Next down is Netzach which is supposed to mean Victory and again, not to be boring, I get no meaning of Victory out of this rendition of Netzach.

This Netzach Sephirah is the sphere of Venus Power or the Greek Aphrodite, which doesn't spell any victory to me.

Also the Sephirah across from Netzach is called Hod which is supposed to mean Glory. This Sephirah is connected to the Greek Hermes or Roman Mercury, and what there is of Glory about Mercury I am again at a loss to comprehend exactly.

I do note that these two — Venus and Mercury — were sometimes considered hermaphroditic. *The Mystical Qabalah* mentions a bearded Venus, and Mercury was noted for his changes especially in the form of Loki the Norse God of mischief, who was always pulling something on the Gods and was forced to undo his tricks which he did many times by changing into a female.

Please note that at the top of the Tree and at the bottom of the Tree we are getting these non-plain sex types. Only in the middle of the Tree is the sex type exactly male or female.

Next to the bottom of the Tree is Yesod which again is filled with conflicting image ideas.

I have always associated Diana, Greek Artemis, the virgin huntress, with Yesod or the Moon and not the symbols as given by Dion Fortune. She is very correct when she says that all the other Sephiroth's Forces are channeled through Yesod, the Moon, onto the Earth. In Astrology, for example, there are certain effects on earth due to certain conjunctions happening. And yet on the day it is due nothing happens and perhaps nothing happens for a week or more until the Moon reaches Full — and then it happens, but it is later than the actual day it was supposed to happen — it takes the Full Moon to "set it off."

And lastly we come to Malkuth. Here is where we are now. One of the titles given by *The Mystical Qabalah* which does make sense is Sphere of the Elements.

Here the Elemental Forces, which entered the top of the Tree as Light, have come to "rest" here as Earth, solid Earth (but it is still Light, not really "solid" at all — it only "appears" solid by a process which I will endeavor to explain in the coming parts of this book. Boy, it will be difficult though! No one has ever been able to do it. But I'll try, and you try to comprehend — hard — work on it with all your perception.)

Dion Fortune says that there are secret tables of Moon tides for Occult workings, etc., which no one knows about except her society. Well, I'm very fond of her, but I don't think this story is quite true. There are no secret Moon tides of any kind that I know of. There are some tides of the Moon, but anyone can figure them out easily. Part is in what I told you already about the Full Moon being the bringer about of the influences of conjunctions of planets which influences are then "funneled" down onto the earth through the Moon and mainly through a Full Moon. There may be tables that she used and which *she* kept secret for her society's use, but it need give you no concern that you are needing anything for your future work.

A sort of summary, then, in order to try to understand ourselves and what surrounds us, including the "clothes" of flesh. Many different religions and philosophies have made their appearance in this Physical World. This second chapter has dealt with one of these philosophies called the Tree of Life of the Caballa. The Tree of Life is merely a system of classifying and listing the elements that make up the Physical Plane World so that they can be seen and understood more clearly and their application to ourselves made plain.

Read and study all the material herein carefully as I plan to expand it right along in the following sections.

As you go along with the material, ponder carefully the parts and points that seem most personal to you and most possible of your personal use for application to the exigencies of your personal existence on this Earth, more especially a happy existence due to no undue confused affairs intruding on your life.

Preface to Chapter 3

In the following section we will study the three "pillars" of the Tree of Life, each in turn.

I first heard of this designation "pillars" in Israel Regardie's book *The Middle Pillar,* although Dion Fortune might have used it, too, but I didn't see it there first. Actually, the word Pillar means just one of the three vertical divisions into which the Tree of Life is divided.

Feeling deeply into consciousness, I note that the three Pillars correspond roughly to the three Fates (see Gayley) of Mythology. The Fates were named Clotho, Lachesis and Atropos. Clotho spun the thread of Life (a person's Life, Lives); Lachesis "twisted" the thread of Life; and Atropos severed the thread of Life at the end.

By straining your romantic imagination a bit you can equate the three Fates with the three Pillars: the first pillar would be the "coming in" (future) into physical existence corresponding to the "spinning" of the thread of Life. A thread is "spun" from a small amount of loose wool by twisting it into a straight line-string of loose wool. This would correspond to Clotho. Then the thread is twisted tighter until it is a real string of wool — the tight twisting would correspond to the middle pillar (present) and to Lacheses. And the third pillar would be the pillar of the past, the result of past physical actions, corresponding to the third Fate, Atropos.

These ideas of correspondences need not be taken too seriously. Just drift into the full idea of looking for general correspondences through life, then make a note of any suggested correspondences for your own intelligent comprehension and future meditations.

Chapter 3
The Three Pillars
1. The Right-Hand Pillar, or the Pillar of the Past

We will consider now the three columns, or Pillars, each in turn. The first pillar to be studied is what I call the pillar of the Past, not known by this name in any other book I've read or found.

The pillar of the Past consists of three Sephiroth, as does the future column; the column of the present has four Sephiroth on it instead of three.

There are three Hebrew Gods connected with the three Sephiroth, which you find on the diagram given elsewhere in this book. There are only two Greek Gods and Goddesses whose names are connected with these three Sephiroth: Zeus, Jupiter, and Aphrodite-Venus. The first Sephirah is called Zodiac only in the Greek connection, but has the Hebrew name as given.

To connect the sphere of the Zodiac, which means, basically, space to move about in, with the idea of the Past is relatively easy. Space to move about in is certainly something that has to "BE," and *be*, be, not be an idea only. "It" has to "BE," there, here, NOW, already in existence, or again, as aforesaid, a place to operate "in," function in. God to function in.

When I use the words "God to function in," we are getting close to another theme of God-action which has opened up to me, and which I am trying to get down on book-paper as quickly as I can. Some of this new (to me) material came in writing this book, but I think I will have to adhere to my original ideas in this book, and save them for the next book, so look for it.

I hope the above will suffice to put in your minds the concepts/ideas of the Zodiac physical space Universe as a place for God (leaving out any question of the idea of the "form" of God) to function in and through.

Also, firmly connect this idea of an, in be-ing Zodiac space, with the idea of Past. PAST.

The composite Elemental symbol connected with Chokmah is Water of Air (page 73). Remember Water. Elemental Force of Water is Condensation, which is certainly a PAST action-reaction, and Air, Elemental Force of movement. So, you have here symbolized a movement in an already prepared place. Space. Which fits the symbolism completely. Please unite yourself with this idea.

The next Sephirah "down" is Chesed, or Water of Fire (page 73), and the Greek God attached thereto is Zeus, or Jupiter, or Egypt's Amoun.

Jupiter governs bankers, speculation developments, gambling and things of like nature, which you can find easily by checking any standard Astrology magazine, and for your own development, I suggest you do so.

Please note that speculation developments, gambling and banking are all of the nature of the PAST. You cannot speculate with something that has not arrived on this plane yet. Bankers must accumulate (past) some wealth before they can operate (bank). And, you must gamble with something accumulated already, so gambling is of the nature of the PAST.

The symbol Fire of Water is accurate here. Water is condensation (past) and Fire is expansion, so we have here an apparent contradiction, but not really. All it means is, there is expansion possibilities based on accumulated resources. Indeed, how can you expand except on some base of some kind? And any kind of a base is a past fact.

Next, we drop down to the last Sephirah on the "bottom" of the column of the past. The sphere of Greek Aphrodite, or Roman Venus (or Water of Water).

Aphrodite rules love, jewels, furs, silks, rich clothes, rich and luxurious things, furnishing, and all such, also

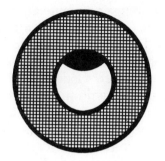

Water of Air

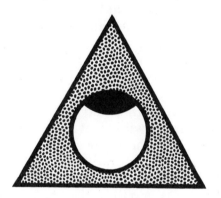

Water of Fire

Water of Water

young people, who presumably are just beginning to learn to "love." All these things are, you can easily see, definitely connected with the past ideas/creations, certainly not anything future. A diamond jewel would have to be created (in existence) before it could be used for anything.

Aphrodite is a female Goddess. There are only two female Goddesses mentioned on the Tree of Life, and they are at the bottom of the columns. The Gods higher up are male Gods, except they do have wives, which wives balance off their male characteristics (except Aries-Mars, whose female counterpart is Athenia, who is more like Mars' sister than wife.)

Also, the lowest Gods and Goddesses are not quite normal in that, both Aphrodite and Hermes are often considered hermaphrodites, and Virgin Diana, many breasted. The reasons for this are rather too deep for this book, but have to do with the functions of the Forces, when they come down lower, taking on multiple characteristics that the "purer" Forces "up" higher had not encountered as yet. Don't concern yourself with it at first, and later, as you grow, you'll come into the knowledge of it.

The symbol for Aphrodite is Water of Water (page 73), and this indicates condensation of condensation. Luxury living is certainly the most consuming base there is. Certainly nothing of much movement in there, or much expansion. Just a "using" base. This concludes the study of the column of the past. Next the column of the Present.

2. The Middle Pillar

Obviously, upon examination, the middle pillar consists of Kether, the first Sephirah, Tiphareth, the second Sephirah — the Sun, Greek Apollo, the second Greek, older, Helios and even ancient Greek, Hyperion. All Suns. Obviously Apollo is the Etheric Sun, or the Etheric "body" of the physical Sun. Hyperion is the real Astral plane "body" of the physical plane Sun.

The next Sephirah is Yesod. The Moon. Greek name, Artemis, Roman name, Diana.

And then, at the bottom of the middle pillar, Malkuth, or Earth. Remember that Earth is divided into four parts, Four Elemental Force parts: Air, Fire, Water, and Earth — Black, Citrine, Russet, and Amber. (?)

As I said elsewhere about the start of Physical Creation, and so I say here, about the symbolic start of this symbolic symbol of the Physical Universe — nothing — not a great deal can be said about Kether. That is, not a great deal of simple things can be said about Kether. The subject is too vast, and definitive knowledge is lacking.

As I have also said, before you can go too far along in the study of the Caballa, you should get *The Mystical Qabalah* by Dion Fortune (she spells it that way. I spell C-A-B-A-L-L-A; same difference.) The book has been going steadily up in price now for some years, but you still need it, as it does contain a vast mass of information about the Occult-Caballa; although the book contains no working plans for "working" the Caballa knowledge. If I may say, with some modesty, I have "dug" up a lot of "workings," and these workings, combined with that book's knowledge should put you far along the path.

So, therefore, I recommend the intense study of Dion Fortune's chapter on Kether, starting on page 109. Also, read the Greek Myths of the Creation by Gayley and what you can make out of that. Also, you might read over Genesis, but remember, it was not written by Moses, but somebody unknown, at or about the time of Daniel, 800 B.C.

So, we will leave Kether and go down to Tiphareth-Apollo.

None of the following is absolutely perfect in its designations. You will have to use your intelligent thought to connect up these various ideas and functions.

To start, the pillar we are now discussing is the pillar of the Present, the nowness — isness — amness — beingness pillar.

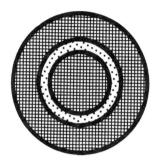

Air of Air

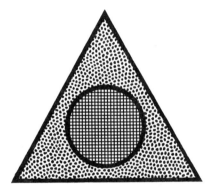

Air of Fire

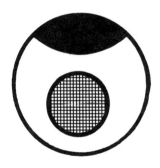

Air of Water

76

Air of Earth

Fire of Earth

Water of Earth

Earth of Earth

Apollo was a God of the present. His activities were all connected with present doings, and things. Apollo was the leader of the Muses and their patron. Please note that songs, dances, poems, and drama are affairs of the present, not future or past. You do not sing a song in the future, nor in the past, but always in the present. And, this idea fits in with the presentness of Apollo, and the middle pillar.

Also, Apollo ruled physicians and medicines; in fact, one of his sons became the great physician Aesculapius. You do not take medicine in the future, nor in the past, but only now. Also, in a close sense, you are healed now, not in the past, nor in the future.

Thus, drugs also are attached to the middle pillar. You don't take a drug in the future, nor in the past, but only in the present, and the effect is also only in the present.

Apollo was not the God of Love. The God Power of Love is the Goddess Aphrodite who, as you know, belongs to the pillar of the past. Love has to be between two already accomplished things, already developed, and of the past nature. However, certain aspects of the love act are of the present, but definitely are based on the past. Remember, I told you these things shaded into each other. Also, Aphrodite and Apollo are brother and sister. There are many other attributions to the present situation so work some of them out yourself, and enjoy it.

We now come down to the sphere of the Moon, called Yesod (read up the Dion Fortune section of Yesod).

I find the Yesod-Moon-Diana-Artemis-Hecate scene very dynamically interesting and glamorous, but you find the part/parts in there that appeal to your Inner Ego and follow that part; do not be swayed by my ideas.

The part of Yesod that appealed to me most was the, to me, startling fact that all the upper Astrological Forces are channelled, or funnelled down on the world through the Moon-Yesod Sephirah. That is to say, clearly, that the effect of any conjunction of planets appears not to take place until the physical Moon reaches Full Moon. Or, in the case of an adverse effect, does not take place until the last days of the dark of the Moon, and over the last hours of the dark of the Moon.

I knew a person who was about to pass on, and he was opposed by the sign opposite his birth sign. I certainly do not go about prognosticating peoples' demises, but as this person was a relative of mine I had a strong "feeling" that the end was in sight, a view which was not held by others, but I did not press my feeling/idea. The person passed on in the last hours of the dark of the Moon when the personal vital Forces are lowest, and the outside opposition of the appearing (today's) sun to the natal sun was highest. However, do not be suggestive, and be swayed by this story. I mean for you to study it only in a general way and see what conclusions you come to in your future living. See if you find any incidence that the effects of an Astrological conjunction is delayed until the Moon is full. And, then the effects of the conjunction are funnelled down on Earth.

There are three Goddesses who rule the Moon, and I would like you to examine their functions. For example, Hecate rules childbirths. There certainly is nothing future or past about the birth of a child. A childbirth is NOWness and no fooling about it.

The elemental symbol for Yesod is Air of Water (page 76), Elemental Air being movability-ness, and Elemental Water being condensation from a former state. So movable-ness of condensing actions is a fair description of the changeableness of the Yesod-Amon Sephirah. Dig out some more for your own knowledge, from the *Mystical Qabalah* and Gayley's *Classic Myths*.

And next we come down to the last of the Sephirah on the middle column/pillar, Malkuth, or the sphere of the Elemental Force of Earth, not Earth itself, please note carefully.

Malkuth is the only Sephirah that is multi-compartmented. Malkuth consists of four quarters, which quarters are labelled Air, Fire, Water and Earth.

Malkuth, therefore, has four elemental symbols attached to it, viz: (page 77) Air of Earth, (page 77) Fire of

Earth, (page 77) Water of Earth, and (page 77) Earth of Earth. As you can see, Malkuth can be readily called the sphere of the Elements, or of the Elemental Forces, as all the Elements come to rest here. You can note that before, the Elemental Forces were somewhat separated from each other, but here in Malkuth, they are very close, and mutual reaction is quite easy.

In the sphere of the Elemental Forces of Malkuth lies the mystery of our physical being — Being. Great and profound statements could be written here at this point of our book, and immense vistas, inner vistas, of philosophic observations and conclusions come to the surface of consciousness, but what good is all that, in a certain sense? What we want is something practical, some practical directions of DOING something about our lives. Or, as the cliche goes, something we can get our teeth into as to how to live this physical life successfully.

In my former books, and in the books to come, I hope, I have presented many "tools," mental and metaphysical tools, for you to use right here and now on this Earth Plane. Many of you have the books, and have made good use of them already. I am not pressure-salesmaning you to buy the books, but that is the only way I have of getting the material out to the world, and to you.°

Each of the books deals with a specific tool of Power, the use of which can enable you to deal with matter, so as to enable you to transcend matter's apparent limitations and come out victorious.

I will give a summary of the books now available, on the market as it were, and describe the "tool" in each book, and thus hope to entice/force you into its use, and for your development, even against your will!!!

The first book I wrote was entitled *The Art and Practice*

_____

° This point in this book seemed such a good place to reintroduce and reemphasize the present books now available that I have broken the continuity of my present book section to do so. I trust this will cause you no shock but that you will absorb the Knowledge and benefit thereby and then return to the present book.

of Astral Projection.

In this book you are given four different methods of "leaving this body-plane" and going elsewhere, where, if you have any drive at all, you should learn a tremendous amount of knowledge/experience about yourself and the inner planes "over there." All true Occult advancement/development consists of some form of projection. The weak sister cat dupes organizations who have nothing on the occult ball, will make all kinds of excuses to *withhold* this knowledge from you, which means that they DON'T HAVE ANYTHING OF VALUE THEMSELVES, and don't forget it. To leave your physical body center of consciousness, and transfer it to your inner sense body/bodies, more or less at will, is an achievement of Occult development which you must eventually arrive at, so why not now? Make the start.

The second book was called *The Art & Practice of Getting Material Things Through Creative Visualization.* In this book, the rules/laws governing the getting of material things through Creative Visualization is laid out as well as Ophiel can cognize them. You are entitled to the best this world has to offer, and don't let any blue noses tell you differently. If you are not getting your share of gracious living, then it is your wrong thinking which is keeping you from getting it. The answers can be in the above-named book.

Also, since writing that book, a great deal of additional information has "come" which adds a vast amount of workable knowledge to the Creative Visualizing concepts. I hope to get this new information down in a new book as fast as possible.

The next book was called *The Art & Practice of the Occult,* and was an attempt to explain some knowledge about the Caballa and the Caballa's connection with the Four Elemental Forces, and other vital knowledge. These knowledge tools are of great value to your working knowledge of the occult as it exists now.

The next book was called *The Art & Practice of Clair-*

voyance. This book shows you how to develop this occult tool for your daily use. You all have this ability now latent in you.

The Oracle of Fortuna was written to enable you to get an answer to a question through the medium of the symbols of the Elemental Forces as embodied in the modified Tarot deck of playing cards. A great deal of illumination can be thrown on a question by these cards.

The last book is called *The Art & Practice of Talismanic Magic* and gives insight into the manipulation of Inner Plane Forces for physical plane leverages "down here."

I hope to write up to twenty-five (25) books, total, before I die so look for them.

This ends the middle pillar.

3. The Left-Hand Pillar, or the Pillar of the Future.

There are three Planes-Forces-Gods on this "future" pillar: Saturn, Mars, Mercury or Saturn, Aries and Hermes, or Forces which are Saturn-Fire of Air; Aries-Fire of Fire; and Hermes-Fire of Water.

You can easily understand the future nature of this pillar when you see/note that all of these Forces are linked with Fire, and you know that Fire is expansion, and you can also reason that Fire/expansion is more likely to be a factor of the future than of the present, and definitely not of the past.

The first God on this future pillar is Saturn, Saturn is an old God, so old that I did notice in several myths, not Greek or Roman, but Nordic and Hindu, that he was referred to by the name Saturn. I am not a history expert, but this did indicate to me some idea of his age in mythology. Also, it seems significant to me that, whereas our days of the week are named after Nordic gods, names such as Tuesday-Twi-Mars, Wednesday-Wodan-Mercury, Thursday-Thor-Zeus, Friday-Friggia-Aphrodite, yet Saturday is clearly Saturn's day, still the same old name, as well as the Sun and Moon (Monday), which two Gods are also probably very old, although why Saturn would be noticed alongside the Sun and Moon (more obvious) is not too clear to me, and the three names Saturn, Sun and Moon do not change with geographical sections/districts, but Zeus, Hermes, Aphrodite, Aries change as aforesaid. As has been said, "What's in a name," but why don't you look this up for yourself, and see the reason for these changes? The research will be good for you.

I remember, in passing, that the age of Saturn in mythology was called the Golden Age (see Gayley). Then no one died, there were no sicknesses, no winters or bad climates. Food grew freely for all. Especially were there no women!!! Procreation was in some other manner. Check your myth books for more details of this age.

You will recall that the wife of Saturn was not too well designated or described. In a number of cases she was called his sister, Vesta!

I have noticed, and mentioned before, that the family relationships at the top of the Tree and at the bottom of the Tree are not too well defined, or delineated sharply.

You will note that there were a number of vague female figures at the creation of the world — Gea, Earth, etc.

And, then at the other end of the Tree we begin to find both Venus and Mercury shown in some type of her-maphroditic form such as a bearded Venus and a Virgin Artemis with breasts! as well as aforesaid half male and half female Mercury.

I can just note this for now — Gayley makes no references to these things. I called up the University of California, in Berkeley, and talked to the Classic Myths Studies Department. I asked about these derivations, and one department member told me there was a classic record series of books in ten volumes in German with thousands of names of connected Gods and Goddesses and related figures! Ten volumes with thousands of names of connected Gods and Goddesses and others; so the answer probably lies in those books somewhere.

As we come down to the general "middle" of the Tree

we find a fairly well designated Wife in Juno, but no clearly designated wife for Apollo, or Mars, nothing but "affairs."

Now, the object of all this digression is to introduce an idea here. Saturn is a male and, as a rule, a male would seem to be a water-condensed past pillar object, and I'd say he was. While, on the other hand, the egg-ovum, with its possibilities, its future possibilities, is surely of the future-fire-expansion.

So, there is a little something wrong here. As I said before, most all, say over 80% of the symbolism is correct, fundamentally correct, so where we have a slight discrepancy here we have to examine twice as hard and deep. Don't be too concerned over this, the answer is hidden for the time being. Saturn is a vague, shadowy figure at best, and I might have done, as the others have done, just overlooked these points and said nothing, but I am not like that. I will give a possible part-explanation. You may recall that I said, in previous writings, that each Sephirah was male to the Sephirah BELOW it and female to the Sephirah ABOVE it.

There is another God Force older than the Greek Saturn, which occupies the same spot as Saturn does but which fills the future functions more clearly than Saturn and that God Force is the Egyptian Isis, the female counterpart of Saturn. For while Saturn is the Father of all, Isis is the Great Mother of All Things. ALL THINGS.

Practically all your life you have heard the words "Mother Nature." Well, SHE-ISIS-IS SHE!! She is the Mother of all.

As the Great Mother from which all (is) to come, she fits the requirements of expansion, Fire, the heart of the pillar of the Future. (Since writing the previous new light/information has come out about the nature of this Mother/Father origin God, which I hope to get out in the next book/books. You can use this knowledge [although, to me at least, not as efficiently as if you knew KNOW the "behind" of it all], so go ahead and use it, but look for more knowledge to come.)

Dion Fortune says something about this matter in a

book called *Moon Magic*, attributed to her, but which, as I note, was printed many years after her death. I find it hard to believe that the manuscript of this book laid around all these years unpublished until recent times. Seems more likely to me that a ghost-writer did this book in her name; not that it makes any difference, and no offense intended.

Also, I hope you are not going to be offended by these little "asides" I am writing/doing all the time throughout these books. I expect to be bitterly criticized and attacked by the "Critics" for my poor layout of these books — that I don't give you their approved conventional system layout — but I am writing to inform you of what Occult basis seems to exist for the transfer of Occult theory to practice. And believe me, that is the most vital necessary aspect of this work — to get the Raw Occult into physical practice.

That out of the way, to get back to *Moon Magic*. She speaks of an "inner temple" wherein was a crude stone statue of a female Goddess, who represented the crude female Forces of Nature, etc. You probably should get this book and study it for what Occult is in it. It just occurred to me, as I was describing Isis, that there was a "crude" aspect and a "refined" aspect of Nature's Forces and the book has some information on it which could be of use to you in your future Magic Power Development and that is what this book is written for.

Also, if I might be allowed to digress for a few more lines here. In one of her books she speaks of a sort of Occult place presided over by a mysterious person, where she lived for a time during the early part of her Occult Career.

What I want to mention is that she speaks of the head of this place (might have been Dr. Taverner in *Secrets of Dr. Taverner*) and says that "he was very secretive in his methods."

I am told the place has been closed for many years, and he is dead and gone, and presumably all his methods and "knowledge" have been lost and not transmitted to anyone. Is this a good idea, to die and leave vital knowledge to no successors? I won't do it if I can help it.

To return to the Pillar of the Future. The Future exists as a sort of shadow world thrown against a kind of a screen, a screen of reverse memory! And, what would reverse memory be? I'd say it was imagination, combined with desire, that makes a picture place, a place where you can project your center of consciousness and move about somewhat, even living, and enjoying the future living to some extent.

Knowing/learning the Tree of Life as you are, learning the Forces connected with it, as you are doing, it should be ultimately possible for you to develop some Power/Direction over your life and thus your future.

Knowing Saturn's functions existence, and Isis' functions existence, and the existence of the Pillar of the Future Forces, should help you greatly.

Now that I think of it, I don't know of any other teaching that even mentions these things and their possibilities. Certainly, the current run of so-called "Rosicrucians" all over the place do not mention such things. I don't want to list them, as it could cause static, but you can check for yourself any time by taking one of their negative, futile courses.

Then again, I cannot tell you *exactly* how to influence and change your future!!

People are all different from each other, and each of you must find the key to his life "lock" for himself and only he can "do" it, and only he can use it.

I'm sorry, but the foregoing statement is much different than you have been led to expect by other teachers, and even religions. They would have you believe that there is a Universal panacea, a Universal answer to a multitude of puzzles. You can see that these things are not true; how could each of our lives be the same, and yield to the same methods and answers?

You are on the right track. You are acquiring knowledge and, knowledge compressed together becomes Wisdom, your knowledge becomes your wisdom, and your wisdom solves your life's problems. That is your job.

So now you know/KNOW the first Forces that exist in the matter of the future, your future. I have not told you all about Saturn and his sisters, and Isis and her husband, Osiris. For heaven's sake seek out more knowledge than I can give you here, about these personified Forces, and assimilate the knowledge into your being, and USE IT!!

For example, I will give one more hint for you to check on in connection with Saturn, and then we will go on to the next God Force, Aries, or Mars.

Every year, around the period just past Christmas, the "old" year is depicted as an old man with a long beard, an hourglass and a sickle. This is one of the depictions of Saturn merged with another version of Saturn called Chronos.

Saturn is old, next to Uranus, the oldest God, but Uranus was somewhat ethereal, whereas Saturn is material. Also present was the sickle, which was Saturn's weapon.

Saturn is also connected here with the idea of Time, and there is a mysterious connection, as it were, with the Occult and Time which has never been resolved. We may do some work on this in the future. Look for it.

Although January 1st is not the beginning of a new year (the NEW YEAR is March 22, the Vernal Equinox), still it appears that January 1st was considered by the Romans, and we picked it up, apparently, from them.

The Romans had a God called Janus, from which our word Janitor comes, who ruled this January 1st date. Janus had two faces so he could look forward and backward at the same time (so can you). Janus is another Saturn! And, now, we will definitely leave the first Sephirah of the pillar of Fire-Future. The elemental symbol for Saturn is Fire of Air or (page 88) expansion of movement.

The next Sephirah "down" the pillar of Fire (sounds like the Holy Roller, or the Pillar of Fire that the Bible said guided Moses across the desert at night) is the Sephirah Aries, or Mars-Fire of Fire, or expansion of expansion, the elemental symbol of which is Fire of Fire (page 88).

Attention is constantly focused on Mars (I think I shall use this name as it is so well known) as the "God of War."

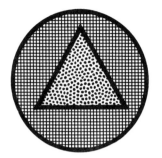

Fire of Air

Fire of Fire

Fire of Water

Heavens! there are a million other things that the Mars Force does that no one ever gives him credit for. Millions of things that I don't even know about, and which I am sorry/glad to say you will have to check out for yourself, and there comes your Occult Growth!

The Police are also ruled by Mars. I don't want to go into this too long and far, but the Occult viewpoint should be known by *use*, and used and supported by you.

Today there is much confusion and hate generated by police departments all over this country, mostly due to the fact that the police and Mars are misused and/or used for the wrong purposes, not really part of their real job, and until this is corrected the situation can only get worse all around. It is rather amazing that the police don't see this themselves, but the Mars Force is very abstruse and non-self-examining, and uncompromising with what it thinks is evil.

I was a child in Iowa City, Iowa, from 1904 to 1915, and when I left there, I had never even seen a policeman. I knew there was a police station downtown, but I didn't know any of the persons there except by rumor, such and such's father was a policeman. Then for many years I didn't see a policeman. Actually, the first time one spoke to me in the goofy tone they use was about 1928, on a trip to Los Angeles, when I started to cross against a traffic light, which I had never seen before, and I was ordered back to the curb by the policeman.

There are a million things that can be said here, but the point is that fat heads in local governments, as well as fat heads in state governments and still larger fat heads in United States government cannot seem to resist the temptation to make Mickey Mouse laws and especially do I mean local city and county governments.

In the old days their Mickey Mouse laws didn't mean too much as a man or woman could go to the local political machine and get these silly things taken care of, including traffic tickets, but as time went on and the cheap political machine and politicians realized the vast income possible through these blackmail traffic laws, for example, they tightened up on their fixing. But all in all it means using the police, not to handle crime, but to handle Mickey Mouse laws designed to bring in filthy lucre only. The laws of Karma are not mocked, or if the fat heads never heard of Karma, there is the American Philosopher Emerson's Law of Compensation, which is also not mocked. The attacks against police will increase as long as the police are used wrongly. I made the preceding language strong to get your attention. Give the matter some study yourself.

While I am painfully aware, and so are we all, that the American Frontier has vanished from America, there are still other fields to explore and conquer. And, it is the Mars Force that is the stimulus for this.

Dion Fortune mentions the digestive processes of the body that break down food and split it up into absorbable forms. This, too, is the Mars Force at work. Also, the processes that change these absorbable forms into heat and energy in the body are types of Mars Forces. (Excuse me, the processes that transform into heat and energy are Mars Forces, the processes that build up tissues are another type of Force, probably a Zeus-type Force — the opposite of Mars. To build up you must have the materials there, available, as it is a past action, a Zeus action.)

To live day by day in an interesting manner and to keep up a lively daily activity requires the successful working of the Mars Force, as you can readily understand, as each new day is a future "coming" to here — coming into here-ness and now-ness.

In this case Mars represents energy, plus desire — desire sometimes called drive, also basically linked with, that horrible word again, Sex, drive.

I rediscovered a little game of solitaire which I called the "Oracle of Fortuna." In this Oracle, the function of the card representing Mars was always a little sort of puzzle to explain clearly. I finally called the Mars card "Energy-plus-desire-to-move, to make a move." So many people, including myself (and mine is increasingly due to older age),

90

use, or invoke, or plan to use, Energy in their life's actions.

Also, again I say the quality of desire enters here. Desire is usually the spark that sets off Energy, so I don't see how they can be separated too far from each other. Please, dear students, check your energy sources and output. Do all you can to clear up the energy outlets at the Physical end, such simple things as adequate sleep, not overeating, etc. Invoke Mars' energy, he is your helper "here on Earth."

Once again, Mars rules the Police, but the rule is to be a right rule, against blatant crime. Notice how the police are used against trivial things, and vast empires of crime are unmolested, such as the Costra Nostra.

In the age just passing away, the Pisces (Hermes) age, Pisces rúled prisons. Society or civilization has a way of trying to put its shortcomings and mistakes, and omissions away into prison hells, and forgetting about them (out of sight, out of mind). But, that age is passing away now, too, and all these are being forced out into the open. Today, September 11, 1971, Saturday, as I write this, there is a prison revolt going on in Attica, New York. And, there was a revolt at San Quentin just a short time ago. These revolts, too, will increase unless the whole matter is taken care of properly. Whether the present fat heads in government can change without being changed themselves is a problem question. Now, you have some ideas about it, and as you grow in Power USE them for the "outside" good. This is the way you can help others, but in no other way for a long time.

Mars, as a Force of the Future, is a Force that can be misused very easily, so for God's sake, be careful about your use of/plans for the Future, as that is where you use the Mars Force.

Hermes/Mercury is the last Planet/Force on the bottom of the Pillar of the Future. As usual, Hermes is the Greek name of this force, and is considered more "spiritual" than the Roman name, Mercury. Mercury was considered more "commercial" than Hermes, and "he" was used/"worshipped" by the Romans as the God of

Commerce. I think the word merchandise comes from Mercury.

I suggest that now that you know about these distinctions, you KNOW and FEEL that you are going to use him when you want to, in both and all his aspects, now that you know about them. All it will require of you to use the different aspects is to know what you want to do, spiritual or commercial, and select your God Force and use it/them accordingly.

Hermes (I will use the Greek name) rules the mind, which means he rules the mental sphere, which sphere is also, I suppose, easily understood by everyone as the mentality.

I would say that the Mind is always verging upon the future, but stimulated by the present, and resting on the fundamental base of the past.

Hermes was known as the messenger of the Gods. In other words he conveyed the contacts, messages, between (the) Gods (which you know now are Forces) and men. Please ponder on this statement more yourself. Picture a man desiring something — remember — recall that all THINGS are attached to some one of the God Forces, which, to repeat again, rules his/her own set of Physical Things.

So then, it follows, naturally, that when man desires any of these different things, or learns to USE any of these things, the action necessary for this desire/use is through the Hermes Force, especially as most of the use/desire would be in the future (all desires *are* of the future — how could there be a desire of the past? Desire of the past would be memory.)

There is a slight discrepancy here. Present use would, of course, be the middle pillar, ruled by Apollo, plus Diana, but remember that Hermes' future becomes Apollo's present very fast. In fact, for all practical purposes, the whole Life Tree Action is instantaneous. We only separate it for examination. Also, in using a thing, as a tool, the use of the tool involves a minute future desire just before each present use, so it does hold together.

The Egyptian form of the Hermes Force was called Thoth, and was a human body with a bird's head, the head of an Ibis. The Ibis had some symbolic significance to the Egyptians as a symbol of Wisdom, which symbolism escapes me, except Paul Foster Case said something about the bill of the Ibis represented a hunting or searching desire connected with "fishing" for ideas, as in meditation or contemplation (not the same). Thus, you will find an Ibis perched on a tree inthe background of the 17th Tarot Card, The Star, which card represents meditation. And, of course, meditation and contemplation would be one of the functions of Hermes, both of these things are very clearly related to the future and definitely not of the essence of the past.

I have explained elsewhere the occult difference between meditation and contemplation, but I think I had better do it again.

To meditate is connected in a sense with the word meditate and means, in this case, to bring two things together, two different things together, such as one of the things being you and the other thing being the knowledge desired. To meditate then means to enter a mental state, on an inner plane, wherein you advance, mentally, toward the object of your meditation, and, presumably, the object of your meditation moves toward you, until you meet, and you acquire the knowledge you want. This is true meditation, and all others you hear about, like transcendental meditation is just a put-on, to cater to ignorant students for some purpose, probably just to get their money. But they can do as they please. All they can lose is a lot of time and money, but that is their right, and privilege, nowadays.

Contemplation, on the other hand, means to enter the inner plane-mental state (not mental plane) with a definite pattern or template — template-pattern-design held in thought — about which pattern you desire knowledge-information-con-with-template pattern.

Thoth-Hermes was also the God Force of all Magical operations as any magical operation is certainly of the future

— designed to change the future (you cannot change the past). So, it will be to the Hermes Force that you will look for help in your magical operations.

Now, we come to another puzzling variation of Hermes-Mercury-Thoth. The Egyptian God Force named Anubis, also connected with the Hermes-Mercury section of the Caballa.

This Egyptian God Force was pictured and sculptured as a man's body with the head of a Jackal! As far as I am aware, this presentation of Hermes-Mercury-Thoth as a Jackal headed man-God is only Egyptian. It did not appear in Greek or Roman Religious functions. I venture here the suggestion that the reason for the non-appearance of this Jackal headed God-form in those civilizations was due to the fact that the Greeks and Romans were not possessed, or shall we say not obsessed, with the kind of death ideas that the Egyptians were possessed with.

This Anubis was known as the guide of the dead through the afterlife (underworld). (I have also run across vague hints that Hermes-Mercury was also a guide of the dead on their way to Hades, or was sent to Hades on missions, etc.)

As you may recall, the Egyptians did have a well-organized idea/system of an afterlife, the main feature of which seemed to be that by paying a writer, called a scribe, to draw up a series of charms, affirmations and denials (much like a Christian Science treatment today) they could cheat or persuade, or bamboozle a whole series of Gods into believing that they were perfect, that they had led perfect lives, and were well deserving of the best of treatment in the afterlife.

As an aside, I find this Egyptian idea refreshing, that a mere man can deceive a God, which idea gives man more importance than the Christian religion, which considers him some kind of a worm.

Also, it introduces another idea that maybe this whole fabric of Physical Plane existence is a fake, and is only what it seems to be because we accept it as so! that after all the

Gods are fakes, in the sense that we believe them to be, and we are the real bosses!! And, it takes only a charm, or an affirmation, or a denial to change things. This idea is in line with our conception heretofore studied many times, that the Gods are Forces, not personalities, although, to repeat again, it makes for easy use to regard the Gods as personalities instead of Forces because of our Physical Plane set-up ideas of Life.

Let us return to today's use and application of Hermes. Thinking and planning are natural future-type applications of the mentality, and as such as ruled by Hermes from his natural position on the Tree of Life, which I hope you begin to understand by now, especially as to the part you play in all this, which, after all, is the object of all this work and study — to show you your part and teach you how to play it but good — and cool.

Conclusion to Chapter 3

The Idea that the Tree of Life pattern is/was based on a past, present, future design was one that I didn't find in the books — but the idea sprang out of somewhere during my studies of and on the Caballa and the Tree of Life pattern.

In closing the preceding section I'm afraid I got a little too broad and sort of lost sight of my main goal in Occult books which is to make the Occult workable, daily workable, *by you*.

However, let us be philosophical about it, and, although attenuated, nothing is lost. Understanding as you now should more clearly, that our physical life is threefold, you can take this threefoldness into account in all your future dealings and use the known Forces as helpers, each in its proper position.

I can give some working directions also — as another old trite cliche has it — Knowledge is Power, vis — when you are first starting your inner plane work, it is of great help to you to use circles, candles, ceremonies, chants, mantrams, etc. BUT as you gain knowledge you control all things by just *thinking* of them. No need of the previous kinds of actions at all.

Preface to Chapter 4

In the pages of books to come we will deal with some new developments that I mentioned have "arrived" since I started writing this book. These new developments pertain mostly to new (to me) knowledge about how the physical universe is constituted, and where the past knowledge and practices, heretofore given, fit into their place.

I am a little disturbed by these new developments, as the new developments might, at first sight, tend to render the "old" knowledge useless, after we have spent so much time learning it (I spent 40 years).

What should happen, however, is that the new knowledge should add increased understanding to the old knowledge and practices, so really they should become more powerful as you know more deeply WHAT YOU ARE DOING.

And, what are you doing? Basically, you have become aware of the existence of planes other than this one. You should have achieved some success with transferring your center of consciousness to your bodies on the other plane, and opened up some experiences there which should have prepared you for genuine growth of self-knowledge, and made you hunger for more, more, more.

In addition, you should have learned a great deal about the NATURE of the Inner Plane substance, and how to manipulate this substance, which is all Magic really IS.

Also, you should have learned the basic ideas of *starting causes* on the Inner Plane, *to make effects come out here.*

Chapter 4
Workings

In writing the book, THE ART AND PRACTICE OF CABALLA MAGIC (during its writing, I mean), Ophiel acquired a lot of additional knowledge based upon "advanced" — in the sense of outward, extended, practices — uses of the Tree of Life Caballa pattern.

I must admit that I got carried away by this overlapping, and put some of this advanced knowledge into this book, where it doesn't make too much sense without the intermediate material fill-in.

I'm terribly sorry about this. My whole inclination is to proceed in an orderly 1, 2, 3 manner. BUT I'm all alone here. There is no one I can consult with, except perhaps my friend, Francis Israel Regardie, and he is very busy with his own work and his own writing and has other concerns, too, in his life. So, as I said, I'm all alone, and these last two books just overlapped and got out of hand.

I can add some more information here, however, before proceeding with the workings part of this book. To repeat, the first book I wrote was THE ART & PRACTICE OF ASTRAL PROJECTION. I never did know just what the reason was for this book's subject. That is, I didn't know until just lately. I had this burning desire to explain the Inner Planes and to accomplish a certain kind of work there. Later, I found out how to accomplish the work I wanted, in another manner, learning the projection part intact (I may repeat this story in more detail in the next book.)

It was through the projection part that I came across the Astral Light. I "saw" the Astral Light on the Inner Plane, and that seeing led off to another search as to what it

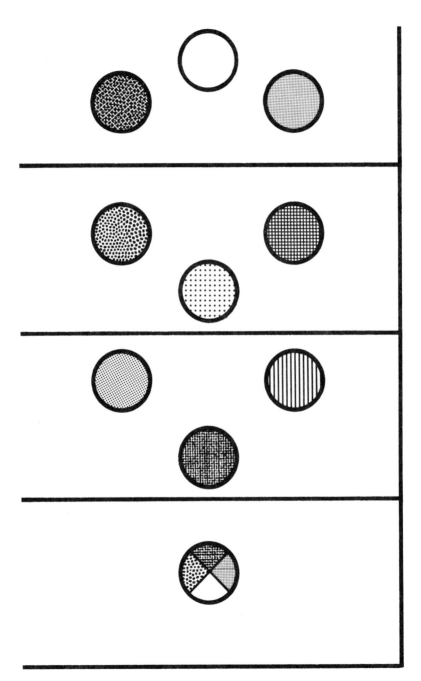

Fig. 1a

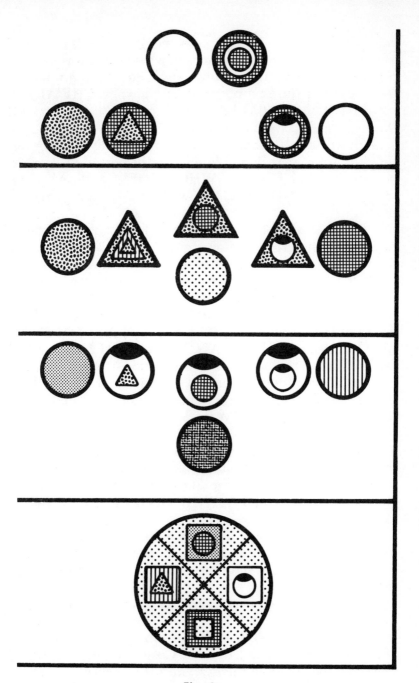

Fig. 2a

was — REALLY — that I was seeing. And, this is the point where I began to get the other knowledge that was in front of what I am presently putting down. So, here I am now. I have to finish this one book, to be known as THE ART & PRACTICE OF CABALLA MAGIC before I can go on with the next book, as yet nameless.

However, all is not lost. In fact, nothing is lost, even though, in the next book I intend, to the best of my pen, to go into the "ONE" IT IS WHO "DOES"; still, what the "ONE" uses to DO with is the "stuff" we are going to study next.

There is another great mystery here, and I have not made much progress in resolving it. To state it as clearly as I can, there is an outer Universe separate from you, and then there is an inner mechanism you have/possess which you use to cognize this outer physical universe, and in so cognizing this outer physical universe you MAGICALLY TRANSFORM something, SO THAT YOU BECOME THE UNIVERSE ITSELF AND EXPERIENCE THE UNIVERSE (I suppose you can call this living.)

This idea/thing is touched on briefly in the "Golden Dawn" books wherein the phenomenon is called "The Magic Mirror of the Universe."

The idea, greatly oversimplified, is that —
a force/forces from "out there" impinges on the outer edge of your sphere, surrounding you, and you transform the force into a FORM, give the FORM movement, expansion, condensation and solidity. YOU GIVE the force BEING, "physical being"!

Now, again I say, I do not know the exact way, or manner, or mechanism, by which this transformation is done, but it is done. And, our/your World/Universe is the result.

Now, we will go back to the study of the nature of the material itself. Remember, there are two things here we are dealing with. First, YOU and your function as a "receptor" and "connector" of, let us say "Cosmic Energy" (?) and, secondly, the "Cosmic Energy" stuff that comes to you constantly in a form being created constantly by either the

Lesser Countenance (Hebrew) or the Demiurge(ous)°
(Greek) for which, see the new book to come.

There are a number of names by which this "Cosmic
Energy" is known. I have said this aforetime so will try not
to repeat it too much in this book. The reason for this diver-
sity of names is that each time some person got out on the
inner planes and discovered this "Cosmic Energy" he gave
it his own name. Apparently, each one never ran across the
names already given to the thing by others, in different
times, and places, nor recognized the qualities of the substance as used and described by others.

We now come to the part where we study the Tree of
Life and the distribution of the above-named Forces upon it
and through it; which distribution constitutes living our
physical life, which is another way of saying the same thing.
(Remember I said elsewhere you, YOU, were a small Tree of
Life Universe, which cliche you hear constantly in the occult, but this time try to absorb its full meaning.

There is another Knowledge point to settle/explore
here (will there ever be an end to these points? No! Never!).
The quite common-sense question arises here — what is the
MATERIAL of which the Physical Universe is made.

I am terribly sorry, but to this question I cannot give a
sensible answer to you who are used to a multiplicity of
different kinds of matter — materials. I will say the apparent truth as best as I can. The Physical World Creator,
whether it is the Greek Gnostic Demiurgeous, or the Jewish
Zavir Anpin, uses elemental essence out of which to create
the "World." And, this elemental essence is itself!!

The only other explanation I can add is that the
elemental essence is in different states of development, and
being in different states of development, can react with
itself. °

° Sometimes this name is spelled Demiurge and sometimes Demiurgeous.

° Remember that each element goes through three stages before it reaches the
final-final state such as Earth of Earth. Earth of Earth is, of course, Physical
Earth and does not react, metaphysically further with itself. However, Physical
Earth is made up of things which do react with each other, but this is not what is
meant here.

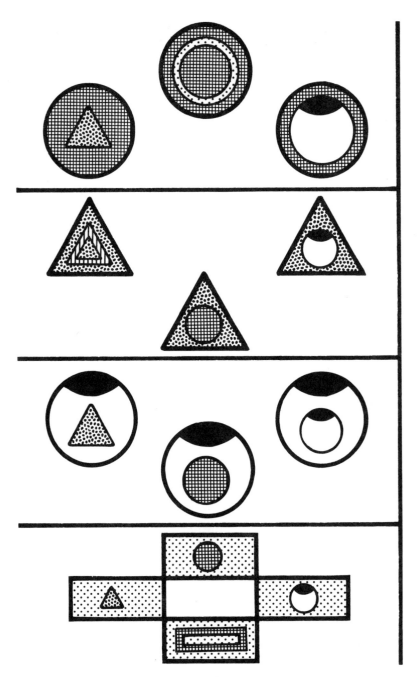

Fig. 3a

We will proceed — draw a Tree of Life, call it Fig. 1a.

This diagram is, of course, the basic Tree of Life symbol. I am trying to have all these diagrams in this book printed in colors. The ideas behind these colors are wildly given according to all kinds of differing color scales which vary from school to school and vary for no kinds of the same reasons so YOU use the colors that appeal to you, and you will probably be as right as any of them and also right according to YOUR personality.

In this Fig. 1a I again introduce the idea of the Future, Present, and Past connections with the three pillars as they have been called by Dion Fortune and Israel Regardie.

As far as I am aware at this time no one else has presented the Tree of Life in this Past, Present, Future manner. I wish someone had so I wouldn't be totally responsible for it.

The colors have some connection with the different states in the development of the Elemental Essence referred to, development from "light" to "heavy" (???). The various colors for the various states of development are given in Dion Fortune's book as referred to heretofore many times. Eventually you should make up a book containing the whole series of "Trees." I find that as I contemplate this color situation and some of its ramifications I realize that the combinations are almost endless and much more than I can get down here in this little book.

You were presented with a study of the three parts of the Tree previously, and it won't hurt to review that part again in detail.

This time we are concerned with the division of the Tree into its elemental constitutents, thus showing how they can react with each other. Draw another Tree, thus: Fig. 2a.

Please note that you are looking at the Tree hence, the two sides are reversed to your two sides, your right and left side, I mean. So, turn around, mentally, and back into the Tree. Once backed into the Tree this puts the Tree, expansion, future side, on your right-hand side.

With the exception of those who are "left-handed" a man starts, or initiates, actions with his right hand, which is in correct line with future-type actions. The left hand holds, or supports the right hand, which action, again, is in line with the idea of past action.

However, what I wanted to develop at this time is the conception of how the "Creator" creates out of himself, which is also the creating material, the created sustained material physical Universe (which is also you).

The preceding ideas are not easy or simple to follow, and I do not present them in the form of a completed thesis, but only as an anology — something like this takes place, but metaphysically, not necessarily physically. You try to put yourself into the feeling of these things, think of these things, meditate on these creation ideas. Contemplate these things until you absorb them.

Look again at Fig. 2a Tree 2. What you see there is a Tree Universe (also small Tree you=Small Universe) in which (also like you) some of the Elemental Essence has already reached the "bottom" of the Tree and become the Elemental Force of Earth, whereas, obviously, at the "top" undifferentiated Elemental Force is entering the Universe Tree (and you) and becoming the Elemental Force of Air.

Please, PLEASE, read the above several times. This knowledge is not hard — the Knowledge is different only — different from earthly knowledge and practice.

The main point is — there is no-thing but God. No-thing besides God. And, therefore all "things" have to be made from — come from — the One Thing — God.

How God transforms itself into these Elemental substances is part of the Knowledge referred to previously, and the Knowledge came before the preceding foundation material was written down, thus confusing me no end.

Ophiel does not claim, again, to have the whole answer to IT ALL. I write what my pen puts down. I never know at the beginning of a sentence what the end of the sentence will be. Ophiel's material can be TESTED, and do test it.

Don't accept it blindly. Test it. Learn to Etheric project. Learn to Creatively Visualize. Develop some clairvoyance. So, that is the test. TEST.

There was one factual point I overlooked in the previous presentation. Take a look at the Tree again: Fig. 1a.

Note: Each of the three (3) Sephiroth triangles has Air, Fire, and Water in it, but no apparent element of Earth, except you can see the word Earth repeated three times. Please note: in this case the Element Earth is represented by the next three lower down Sephiroth!!!

There is another clue for you available as to how God can use itself to react with itself. Look at Fig. 2a.

Please note that in place of the round circles, Sephiroth, I substituted the Elemental Force's symbols in combination with each other.

Most of this material was given in my book THE ART & PRACTICE OF THE OCCULT. Opposite page 84 of THE ART & PRACTICE OF THE OCCULT is a page of combination Elemental Forces, in this case including Akasha.

I hope it is becoming clearer to you HOW the Elemental Forces can react with each other, even though they are more alike than not alike.

And these then are the building blocks of the (apparently) solid physical Universe (made of Forces which you make real). What power it is that does this I will treat in the next book, as I have to lay foundations in this book first.

1.

Call your attention to the diagram in Fig. 3a. I expect to open up more knowledge and WORK in the next book, but for now please look at, and give some hard quiet thought to, the lower part of the diagram, as that is where we are now, and where we will be for some time, AND WHERE WE WILL WORK FOR SOME TIME, until we transcend it all!

Therefore, in strict accordance with my policy of making all these books your working books, with operating directions, here are the *operating "secrets"* for the preceding three pillars, and the diagrams thereto appended.

In the preceding three Pillars chapter I described the various symbols for each Sephirah, and also included colored plates of each.

Dion Fortune, and others, have given this much in references, or a few scattered plates, such as those in Israel Regardie's "Tree of Life" facing page 128, but no real directions as to how to USE the symbols, especially on and for the Earth Plane. So. Here goes.

Return to the first book, THE ART & PRACTICE OF ASTRAL PROJECTION, and turn to the Symbol Method on page 75. (At the time the book was written the prices of the supplies were relatively low. Now they have gone so high I cannot carry them anymore. Try your local 10c store first, and in most cases they can serve you.)

At first it will probably be all right to use the symbols as given in this book, but if and when you take up real serious work, you should draw, paint, and make your own, and eventually, draw and paint them on parchment, real parchment, which is as expensive now as it was a thousand years ago.

So, I will proceed, assuming you have the symbol in one way or another. Follow the directions as given in the Symbol Method.

For now, when you project through the, in this case, composite symbol, you should find yourself on the plane of that God Force. Move carefully, and explore your way quietly. That Plane is the sphere of the Force that rules what you are interested in, and are working on. You should feel the Boss. If you don't feel like the Boss, then don't enter the plane to do any work until you do so feel, or have gained enough knowledge to handle the operation.

Gaining the necessary feelings of being the Boss and gaining the necessary knowledge are matters that I cannot help you with directly — you have to do that yourself; make your own development.

I would suggest, however, that you first explore the four Elemental Force Planes through these symbols as a means of getting the necessary knowledge and experience.

As I read this book over, and especially these sections (and today and the next two days are the dark of the moon, but don't you become suggestive just because that is the way the dark of the moon affects me — it might only be suggestion with me, too — I want to allow for that also), I am having a little damp dull feeling about the force-value of the book. I want to give you strong occult directions, **and** always, in each new book, open up new paths to Power, as another old cliché has it. Actually, in the books up to now, you have had IT. You got the Basic-Basic. NOW is USE. DEVELOPMENT, and THAT, to a tremendous extent, depends on YOU, and your devoted application in your future. I trust you see this.

In other words, the time is now coming, and may be at hand, when I have given you *all* the detailed techniques — now comes their *use*. And, I am wondering, will my future giving consist of essays on the Occult instead of detailed technique instructions? Your magical work, after you assimilate the opening parts, will consist of your growth, based on emotion desire, sometimes miscalled WILL.

I am not trying to get you all excited about the next book, as if this book is not so hot, but I, myself, have reached another step/plateau into which I was "dragged" by a growth process of elimination (contradiction of terms?) and, in the last year, a whole new "inner vista" has presented itself, and my own personal work "led" (hate that word — implies something is doing some leading!) straight to the Gnostics, and their ideas, which fit in with all that has gone on before.

Students, I'd like to write twenty-five books on the Occult before I pass away. I want them ALL to be good for you, and not pot-boilers. I'm trying not to slip, but if I should, take it easy, will you? I say this and then it will probably never happen, as it is always the unexpected that gets to me.

As we are on the subject, I might as well announce the next two books here and now. I do this merely as an idea of a notification of convenience, no pressure. There should be a book tentatively called WHAT YOU NEEDED TO KNOW ABOUT THE OCCULT, BUT COULDN'T EVER FIND OUT, and this book should be followed by the Gnostic book, title undetermined as yet. Writing has started on the first book, but none on the Gnostic book.

Also I'd like to call your attention to a number of interesting, I think valuable, little essays on Occult subjects which are now available. I call them Occult Vignettes. You will find the present list in the back of this book. These Vignettes are now in copy-type form, but they should be in pamphlet by the time you read these words.

2.

I call your attention to the appended Tree of Life diagram in which the Sephiroth are depicted as compound Elemental Force Symbols instead of in the usual single Elemental Way (Fig. 3).

Also, I call your attention to the section in the first book THE ART & PRACTICE OF ASTRAL PROJECTION called the Symbol Method. Those of you who have read the astral projection book by Yram (Mary spelled backwards. Why?) may recall that Yram gave no great detailed directions as to HOW he (?) managed to project, but did state that his projection was by the Symbol Method. I was quite angry and upset when I read this, years ago, as I then didn't know what the Symbol Method was — not yet having acquired the Golden Dawn books edited by Dr. Francis Israel Regardie (which books you should eventually own for research and reference, so save up your pennies.)

However, to get on with the working of these Forces depicted on this Tree of Life diagram. You should know from your study and meditation of and on the material given in the book, entitled THE ART & PRACTICE OF CLAIRVOYANCE, that each Sephirah has connected with it a number of human activities of a special kind.

As I said you will find the list, more or less complete, in

the aforementioned book, and you can supplement this list by looking at ordinary Astrology books and magazines.

So, now you know some "different" kind of knowledge which Dion Fortune did not give to you — you know the Tree is divided into Future, Present, and Past types of actions — so be governed thereby accordingly; you know that all the actions that make up the physical plane are connected to some certain Sephiroth; and you know that each of these Sephiroth is symbolized by a compound symbol. You know that there is only one material in the physical cosmos, and this ONE material therefore can react only with itself, and this reaction is only done by different parts of the material ACTING in a different manner from other parts of the same material, but still being the same basic material — you can use the idea of different vibrations of the same material if that idea is clearer to you.

Remember the four kinds of Forces, or, to repeat, the forms of vibrations that Forces take: Air — movement, movability; Fire — expansion; Water — Condensation; and Earth — stability, inertia.

Now, with that review out of the way we can proceed with the how/use. We will assume you desire to acquire something, or to become something pertaining to the nature of, and ruled by Jupiter/Zeus, or as you now know — Water of Fire (See Fig. 3a).

We will assume you have done the usual kind of working/visualization, maybe a Talisman, which should have this compound symbol on it, etc.

Now comes the heavy heretofore unknown "secret" from old times — a combination of two occult devices or techniques, creative visualizations and symbol method projections.

You were given the method of symbol projection in the first book, THE ART & PRACTICE OF ASTRAL PROJECTION, but I will repeat it here with some additions.

Following the above idea of using the symbol of Water of Fire, which you should make for yourself, you place the symbol in front of you, in a good light, and look at it steadily for a few minutes. Then turn your gaze aside onto a piece of white paper. You should then see the symbol in complimentary colors on the white paper. Then close your eyes and you will again see the symbol against your inner sight background. When you see this inner symbol, then seize the symbol, this comes with practice, and enlarge the symbol in your *imagination*, expand the symbol until it becomes as large as a door, in simmering complementary color. Then project or step through the curtain/door.

Where you will find yourself is where the Forces/vibrations of what you want or are interested in, are at.

The rest is up to you. Be careful and explore the place carefully, and make your requests/demands carefully. This part is something you will have to do for yourself, as I cannot do it for you. But move carefully and quietly.

Also, you can use the same method on any article which is in the nature of a symbol — a picture, a drawing, a trademark. Follow the same method as outlined. One of the objects of this operations is to put you in tune with the vibrations of this "place." The Place where the object is "ruled" by the vibrations which "control" the object of your desire. I repeat, you are to be brought into the aura of the object of your desire.

Now, also, I guess I'll spill another occult "secret." When you use a trademark, or something else solid and three dimensional then, in addition to looking at the object, you also feel and handle the object and add the psychometry effects to the vibes you are building up in connecting yourself to the object. In other words instead of "reading" the object as you would in psychometry, you feel/ally yourself WITH the object and all it represents to you.

Please note how these different occult techniques blend into each other. I may write separate Vignettes on these subjects later.

3.

Return your attention to the combination diagram
(Fig. 3a) — the combination diagram of the ordinary Tree
of Life Sephiroth circles with their symbol combinations.
You will notice, in this diagram, that the Tree of Life has
been set up in a certain way — the three pillars have been
designated the Elemental Forces of Air, Fire, Water. The
central pillar is labeled AIR, facing the diagram, the right-
hand pillar is labeled WATER, the left-hand pillar is labeled
FIRE.

(Hah! you ask where is Earth, the elemental force of
Earth? In the case of this diagram, the elements change-pass
from one element to another, and as a rule the element
below can be considered "earth" to the element above. The
line of change can also be considered the element Akasha,
which is not shown here. When you make your diagrams,
you can insert the Akasha symbol on the line if you wish and
color it Indigo.)

Now look at the other division of the Tree of Life.
Notice that the diagram of the Tree of Life is divided into
four horizontal sections, three sections of three Sephiroth
each, and one section of one Sephiroth divided into four
symbol sections. The main sections are cross-labeled Air,
Fire, Water, Earth. And the single Sephiroth in the Earth
section is also divided into four symbols of Air, Fire, Water,
and Earth (indicating that all the elements are present in
Earth).

Now having got ahead of myself I will have to go back
and fill in. The building blocks of the Physical Universe are
the four (five) Elemental Forces. To repeat — Elemental
Air, Elemental Fire, Elemental Water and Elemental Earth.
These Forces are Real but not "Real" (great mystery here,
see my other writings). BUT you LIVE and ACT as if these
Elemental Forces were "REAL."

The Sephiroth, on the Tree, *are* the Elemental Forces,
and they create and build up and constitute the physical universe by acting and reacting on and with each other. As you
know, because I have said it elsewhere, the undifferentiated

Elemental Essence, known as Akasha, comes into the Physical Universe from beyond Kether and then takes on the characteristics of each of the Elemental Forces in turn as it descends "down" to Earth.

It would appear that the first arriving Force having gone on down and become some more advanced form would then act and react with later arriving Forces, let us say lighter Forces. And, as I said, these actions and reactions form the Physical World. For clearness it could be said that as soon as the Forces began to differ from each other in qualities they can then react with each other to form combinations of qualities which combinations constitute all Physical Things according to manner, plus position on the Tree.

Therefore look again at this diagram. Each Sephirah has, along side of it, a compound symbol. This compound Elemental Force Symbol is the Elemental Force Symbol for that Sephirah. Ponder and meditate on this HARD. The WAY these Forces are USED is through the symbol and is as follows. (Of course you should have a deep reason for using the system, and you should make positive preparations well in advance for the operations — much information is contained in the Golden Dawn Books, the information parts, not the ritual parts.)

To continue. To use. You first decide exactly what it is that you want to do/accomplish in regard to what subject (in the world) you are interested in. You then study and select the Sephiroth/symbol pertaining to that subject. You then draw and paint that symbol on a 4" by 4" card. Check the proper colors, but you select the color that appeals to you among the shades available. For example, there are a number of reds, from cardinal to crimson, and the one YOU select is your YOUR/COLOR.

When this preliminary work is completed, you proceed as follows. Select a comfortable position. Shine a light on the card-symbol. Look at the card for a time, but do not do so for so long as to strain your eyes. After a time shift your gaze to a plain piece of paper. You will see the symbol on the plain piece of paper in complementary colors.

Shut your eyes, and you should then "see" the symbol on the back of your eyelids, as it were.

Enlarge the symbol in your imagination and then step through it.

You should then find yourself INSIDE the plane of that symbol, and you should then ACT ACCORDINGLY, and that is not what I can tell you how to do exactly. Your actions then depend on the preparations that you made previously and what you want to accomplish with the forces on that plane. (See my other writings and the suggested courses that lead to Illumination and, for want of a better word, POWER to function on this Earth Plane through the Knowledge of the descending forces of the Inner Planes.)

Chapter 5

What you should have gotten from the first part of this book was more basic Knowledge about the Caballa ideas/system. Actually, there is a tremendous amount of other material written down, but I have not pursued it because I have felt that much of this material was redundant, and also, much of this material was speculative, and the rest was a philosophical dissertation of the nature of the middle-ages debates on how many angels can dance on the point of a needle, etc.

I feel satisfied to believe that I got a set of Knowledge/Workings out of the Caballa which, while not ALL by any means, will DO until more comes along. That is, will do for most any and all kinds of necessary work you need, or want to, or have to do, on this physical Plane.

Oh, there are "higher things" indeed, and I shall never cease to pursue the higher things and get them down on paper/books for you, but the higher things will not add more to your present basic workings.

It is somewhat as if you were to consider the driver of an automobile. As a driver you have a good use/control of the automobile. You do not need to be an automobile engineer in order to operate the car. In fact, an automobile engineer might not be a good car driver at all. But, if you want to graduate from an automobile driver to automobile engineer, there is no reason you should not do so, but many will not choose to so do. The above layout sounds rather inverted, but it is true nonetheless.

So, with this clearly understood, we can proceed along the lines of Knowledge, with no fear that something is being neglected or overlooked, or left out.

We have, up to now, been studying how to accomplish

changes on this plane through various kinds of leverages, mental leverages and metaphysical leverages, and magical leverages; the only thing is that as we go "higher" we come closer to the SOURCE of all mental, metaphysical, and magical leverages; the much more direct SOURCE from which ALL pours out from, and theoretically, the necessary work/power should become easier and easier, say, once we near the SOURCE we would not, for example, have to make a Talisman to accomplish a certain object, we would proceed to do it directly by being near the SOURCE.

I have not completed my studies of the SOURCE, indeed hardly started the studies, and I will do no more than hint here, and say I will try my best to get it in the next book, but will tie up all the loose ends I can here and now; and even if I am not able to write the next book, you have enough knowledge and workings here and in previous books to carry on all you need.

So therefore, to proceed, we will start this part with the statement that while we *know* there is a higher SOURCE, as aforesaid, what we now are dealing with is a complex of Forces and Powers BELOW this SOURCE. Below means below in point of origin.

There was an old-time author many years ago, and read by me many years ago. (I thought, memorywise, that I had in mind Judge Thomas Townsend's book, "The Hidden Power," which you should read for your education. He was a metaphysical mystic, not magic, but on re-examination I do not find the statement in his book, I was looking for).

At any rate, my memory says an old-time occult author said, -as follows: "There is no-thing, nothing, in this Universe, no material but God (material) in existence." Therefore, speaking broadly, in this *material* universe there *are* many different things; things differing from each other, yet all these different "Things" are the same one Thing, in basic actuality. All different Things are the same thing in reality, sourcewise.

Let us use an old cliche. Physical things differ in different shapes/appearances from each other, because each has different vibrations, each operates on a different wave length, which wave length causes a different appearance of each same/different looking *THING*!!!

After you have digested the preceding we can go on. As there is nothing but God (material) in the Universes (non-physical and physical; above Kether and below Kether) All, everything(s) is no-thing else.

I can digress here for a moment. In the next book we will go into the matter of the kind of material there is in the universe (and I may repeat this whole paragraph). Here I just want to mention in passing that different Gnostic systems postulated the existence of TWO SUBSTANCES in the Cosmos. And, these two substances were called LIGHT and DARKNESS, and so on. The two substances system was called, naturally, Dualism (which idea never entered my head before).

With that idea out of the way there is another concept we must contend with, and that idea/concept is, IS MATTER REAL? Really real?? Or, an "Illusion real?"

I can give an answer to this, saying simply, matter is not really real (even physical physics shows that physical matter has more holes than material in it), but we should act as if matter is REAL, but keeping the truth in the back of our minds at all times.

Therefore, then, the Physical Plane World must be established so that it *appears* hard and solid, acts as if it is hard and solid, and deceives all human beings into thinking that it is hard and solid. How can such a Universal illusion/delusion be brought about?

Well, it is no great secret. The Physical Plane solid illusion creation is accomplished through the deployment of the senses, plus the employment of the Five Elemental Forces; reacting with and on each other, and thus creating a solid appearing world.

In more detail: You "arrive here," on this earth plane, equipped with five senses in embryo. You grow up, and the physical plane world expands through/to your senses. In the diagram you are the five-pointed star, and each point is a sense, a physical sense. Your senses form a sphere around you (somewhat analogous to the sphere of availability as given in the book, "The Art and Practice of Getting Material Things Through Creative Visualization.") This sphere has been much overlooked in magic Knowledge; an occult secret left out in the open freely, and thus "hidden" as, indeed, most all occult secrets are likewise so in the open and hidden by this obviousness!!!

Outside the egg-shaped (I didn't make it too well egg-shaped) magical mirror are "raw" undefined, undelinated, vibration type, layer type, thought form types and shapes, and just plain FORCES, which FORCES, shapes, thought form types, layer types, vibration types, undelinated, un-defined "raw" Force Pressures are CONVERTED into the objects and THINGS of the Physical Plane; YOUR physical plane, which makes up your physical world by you. In other words, you make the non-solid (?) SOLID, the non-material MATERIAL — YOU DO IT — YOU ARE THE MAGICIAN IN THE ONE TAROT CARD!!! And, I repeat, you do it by means of the magical Power in your five senses.

Another aside. As to who you/we/I am/are EXACTLY, I am not prepared at this time to designate exactly, and define in precise terms what and who we were or are, or how we got here, or what the hell we are doing here, and why don't we remember anything as to aforeness, etc.?

I have a few rather weak ideas, but if I go around saying/talking weak ideas, then some people will jump on that saying, and resay, "See, I told you Ophiel knew nothing!!" I don't think any *human being* will ever KNOW ALL ABOUT IT HERE. With any kind of a little bit of luck I hope to have some stronger ideas as to who we are in the next book; at least I will have what has been spoken/written up to now by saints and sinners, and maybe we can go on from there.

So, leaving out the great questions of who we are, we go on to where we left off; you are the creator of the/your physical magic mirror universe, through your magical five senses. As might be said, in thinking you are perceiving the physical universe you are, in reality, doing the opposite of perceiving from out to in, you are projecting in to out the physical universe!!

Now I realize that the preceding leaves unanswered more questions than it answers, but remember I do hope to write more and more books, so let's leave something for later. Learn the present knowledge well, and then the foundations for more knowledge is laid. Again, I repeat the main object of the past books, and this present book, and the books to come, is to give out hard workable knowledge, and to work the Caballa Magic. You do not need to know it *all* now.

All you have to *know* for now is that it is through the POWER of the ELEMENTAL FORCES, which you possess, in your five senses, that you control and create the Physical World-Plane, which surrounds you.

Look at the next diagram in this book. I have replaced the conventional circles with symbols. Please note the symbols carefully. You will recall I told you that there was only one substance in the universe above Kether and below Kether. This statement is true. However, you *know* that here on the earth plane there are different substances; yet you also know that each of these different substances are composed of the same basic things; electrons and what is beyond electrons.

Or, as can be said in another way, a/one basic substance reacts with other parts of itself to make different combinations of itself, which combinations react with each other to constitute the physical plane world. However, do remember the substances referred to are FORCES acting as if they were substances, reacting with your senses, and thus creating the *illusion* of solid substances.

You should now have some ideas as to what IT is all about; the physical plane I mean, and you. Your employment of the Elemental Forces in combinations is your/you creating your world.

Again I say, a million questions are not answered here, but some light has been thrown, and you should be able to get on with living and even progressing.

I can see that I am running out of material for this book, as all points to the theme of another book, the nature and contact of the Demiurgeous, who apparently is the "maker" of these elemental Forces we are studying (but does not constantly supervise their USE, YOU do that, as aforesaid; EXCEPT — possibly — in some cases "it" can be influenced in definite ways, as presented in "The Art and Practice of Getting Material Things Through Creative Visualization).

Chapter 6

Here is an easy way to make Tree of Life diagrams with paths. When made paint the diagrams in the King scale and in the Queen scale. Also, the paths in the King and Queen scale.

I am not satisfied completely with these colors, nor the ideas behind the colors. To be absolutely, plainly open, I have not found a blinding explosion of Divine Revelations behind the colors, or indeed any Power attributions to any system of colors, that seem to produce any kind of results, hard-core results, on this Physical Plane.

I have not been able to find out where these color ideas came from originally, or what "working" significance they really have. I sometimes feel that these colors are as screwed up as much of the Occult is.

For example, it seems as if the color of Kether — white, or absence of color — sounds correct. Also Chokmah — Gray. This Sephirah is beginning to take on some matter-substance, therefore the former white is tinged with matter, hence gray.

Now we come to Binah — the sphere of Saturn. The color for Saturn is black. Now, this is very funny — funny, however, in the sense of being strange, not in the sense of amusing — quoting Noel Coward from the play "Blithe Spirit!"

Black is also the color of "coal tar" from which *all other colors* can be made, by chemically treating coal tar.

Correlate this fact with the idea that Saturn is the ancestor of all the family of the Gods. In other words, ALL comes from through Saturn.

There is another idea/conception/color connected with this Binah-Saturn Sephirah. It is taught, and I have accepted it because it hangs together, that each Sephirah, and the Gods/Goddesses connected with it, are positive to the Sephiroth BELOW it and negative to those Sephiroth ABOVE IT. Or, another way of saying it is, male-positive to what is below it, and female-negative to what is above it, or, there is a connection with each Sephirah.

There should be two colors connected with each Sephirah, a positive male color, and a negative female color.

The male color of the Sephirah of Saturn is Black, and the female color is Indigo. The female Goddess is Isis, the Great Mother of All.

These ideas also hang together, because Isis is the Great Mother of All Things, from which all things come, and Indigo is a vegetable dye from which all colors come from, too, analogous to all colors coming from Black tar. So the symbolism hangs together. So, you can safely assign the two colors, Black and Indigo, to Binah.

Now, when we come down to the Sephirah Geburah — the Sphere of Jupiter-Zeus is blue, and we don't find a color assigned to the Goddess Juno, Jupiter's wife.

Juno did have a totem bird assigned to her, the peacock, which certainly has plenty of color in its body. This is all I can come up with, however. Do you have any ideas?

It would seem, somewhat logically, that the complementary color to blue should be the color assigned to Juno. The complementary color to blue is orange, but orange is the color of Hod/Mercury which is a bit confusing. The solution probably lies in the correct shade of blue. You cannot help noticing that there are a number of shades of blue — from dark blue to light blue — and, for each shade the complementary color varies, too. Probably, for your own individual work, you should explore and discover the correct shades of these for your own personal USE.

So, paint the two Trees in the main color for one, and in the complementary color for the other.

To close this section, I also note that there are shades of red, from dark crimson to light. Also, shades of Green and shades of Orange.

The Moon does seem to have one shade of Violet only. Even in Hollywood, when they want Moonlight in the studios, they use a Violet-Lavender screen over the floodlight.

These colors are a puzzle/mystery. No-one "teacher" now living among those I have studied and contacted can give me any valid Knowledge/Information on the color ideas that I can use or convert to Power uses of the present-nowness. The reason I give them to you now, here, is to get them out of the way so we can proceed along the path, even if the path is not so exact, knowledgeable, and exact as I'd like it to be. Use the colors, and the shades, that appeal to YOU, make you good and RIGHT, as Fire — Mars, Red; Air — Zeus, sky blue; Gold — Apollo, Yellow, etc., for NOW.

Never forget for an instant that YOU are the/that Tree of Life, and that all those Forces — Astrological Forces — are IN you, and coursing through you every second of your physical existence. My teaching "job" is to tell/teach you this fact; to become aware of this fact, and to make a strong effort to USE this Fact as quickly as you can in your life (the use of these facts becomes an ART — the ART OF MAGIC).

Also, these Astrological Forces become the actual Physical World-Plane through the agency of the Elemental Forces into which they transform ?????????

Chapter 7

The Nature of the Inflowing Force. Apparently the whole Physical universe is sustained and maintained by the Inflowing Force from outside the physical universe.

I must apologize that I do not "get" all the full "revelation" about this inflowing Force at once. I hate this piecemeal stuff, but that is the way it comes to me.

I have long given up the idea that any revelation finding was final, although at/in my early times/writings I thought it was, and so indicated, for which I now apologize in every position imaginable. For heaven's sake NOW absorb all this material, the material already given previously — and the material in this book. AND USE IT — BUT BE PREPARED FOR MORE — MORE — MORE in the future. The future material, of which I am as yet ignorant, should add more enlightenment, not less, to that already given.

For example: (1) I have had access to some high-grade Knowledge from Jewish sources; (2) Previously I was guided/led into an examination of Gnostic literature as summarized in several old books, in which summaries I discovered the demiurge, the Gnostic half-God who, I first thought, acted as a governing contact agent between the non-material first cause God, and the material world; (3) Now, I am presented with the idea that this Demiurge half-God, that is half physical — half non-physical, created the Physical World. (Of course under some kind of direction from the First Cause), which idea was not in the/my original conception of the Demiurge; (4) Now, in translating these concepts down to my/our daily life living, I have found a number of vital ideas, which ideas suggest working techniques for us.

These techniques are what is really important to us. Techniques that we can USE to bring about desirable changes in our daily lives, so that we can regulate our daily life in an intelligent manner.

I have given you a great deal of these Techniques now, in my previous books. The use of the Techniques outlined in those books should put you pretty far ahead, for a starter.

As some of you may be reading my books for the first time, I feel I should give a list of these books and a brief description of their contents here, so you can have an understanding of what went before, and bring yourself up to date.

Please believe me when I say I wrote these books with a certain "layer" of thought consciousness in mind. Now I find, that while they do contain that certain layer I had in mind, they also contain germs of a deeper layer of more advanced thought-ideas, which I was not aware of when I first wrote the book.

I hope this doesn't sound too goofy to you. I don't fully understand it myself, but that is the way the cookie crumbles (saying probably outdated by the time you read this!).

But, while I call it to your attention, don't flutter about it, but read the books like fast! GET the DATA and USE the DATA for your life's benefit.

(For those who are reading my book for the first time — others skip.) In my first book, "The Art and Practice of Astral Projection," I gave four rather simple methods of leaving this Physical place/plane and exploring other "places." I now know that this book was given to me — that is the idea was pushed onto me to do the book in order to enable people to, not only explore as much of the Inner plane as they were capable of doing, but THIS EXPLORATION RESULTED IN STUDENTS BEING ABLE TO "SEE" ASTRAL LIGHT FOR THEMSELVES, WHICH ASTRAL LIGHT IS THE DEMIURGE ITSELF, MADE VISIBLE. This seeing was accompanied by some new discoveries which made me realize that there were more details to come. Some details HAVE COME, and I will pass them on to you as fast as I can get them down and published.

The second book was called by the long title, "The Art and Practice of Getting Material Things Through Creative Visualization."

In this book I nailed down the basic concept, my basic concept of Occultism, which is — Occult Knowledge should be of USE TO YOU, FIRST, ON THE LOWEST PLANES, and then, and then only, go on to the higher planes, whatever that/those are.

This book, "The Art and Practice of Getting Material Things Through Creative Visualization," does point out a method of utilizing your Powers to bring about improved material conditions in your life, however, the methods, while they do work, do not explain in detail HOW they WORK, and I always did want, those details *in more exact form.* (As I said, more material is forthcoming in the future books as fast as I can get it down and printed). However, USE this book's directions, and you should get satisfactory starting results.

The next book was called, "The Art and Practice of the Occult," and I see now, was a starting introduction to the Tree of Life, the Elemental Forces, and compound Elemental Forces, and their uses in a practical manner. So, go and do.

The next book was called, "The Art and Practice of Clairvoyance," and was intended to bridge the gap in your personal consciousness between you and the Forces, Astrological Forces, that flood the Physical Cosmos, and to link the Forces up with yourself so you could use them in your daily life-living.

The fifth book was called, "The Oracle of Fortuna," and was a "little" divination system designed to build up a link in yourselved with the basic-basic Forces in the Physical Universe as embodied in the Tarot Card, re-translated into a deck of ordinary "playing cards."

The sixth book, now just out of the throes of publica-

*tion, is called, "The Art and Practice of Talismanic Magic,"
and is designed/written to give you an understanding of
how to link yourself to the Cosmic Forces around you in an
intelligent, controlled manner, through the old talisman's
idea systems.*

*This seventh book, now in the real throes of being
written, probably to be called, "The Art and Practice of
Caballa Magic?" will contain further Caballa Tree of Life
knowledge of a gradually increasing kind. You have this
now.*

*These books, and the others hopefully to come, are for
your benefit. I suggest you get them and, not read them, but
study them hard.*

Dear Students: I criticized Crowley, and others, for not
producing clear and concise, and coherent texts of Occult
material, and now I find I am doing the same thing myself,
but apparently I recognize what I'm doing, and calling your
attention to it while THEY never did. I do hope to connect
all these different sections together properly, but if I don't
make a beautiful connection, then absorb the different sections themselves, as each is valuable and workable.

I guess a summary is in order, both for you and for me:
What I am trying to do, or being led to do, or being kicked
into doing, is to expound a system, or part of a system, of
thinking, acting, and doing, of dealing with the Forces, the
Inner Forces, that make up the Cosmos, physical and
otherwise, so that you YOU can and will be able to start to
control yourself, and control your circumstances.

I make no doubt that there are many ways of doing
this, many systems, and, as the cliche goes, "Many Paths."

I cannot do them all, nor do I even want to know about
them all, or even know about many of them, as the ideas
and symbolism are different in each, although basically the
same. It would seem logical that in the beginning one
system, and one system only, should be followed up by a
student until a degree of proficiency is acquired, and then
the other systems will fall into place naturally.

In my books, and in this book, a sort of Caballa system

has been followed. The system of The Tree of Life diagram.

To make a long story/search longer, my studies into the bypaths surrounding this Tree of Life diagram, plus "Astral Projection," plus "Creative Visualization," has led me personally to a re-re-re-discovery of the/an Astral Light, which led me on back to some fragments of Gnostic teachings/literature/concepts (?) of a half-demi-half-urgeous (God?), who deals with the physical world in some mysterious manner, but which manner can be learned by you, and duplicated by you to a fair degree, by hard work and dedication, to a more satisfactory degree.

This, then, is what we have done up to now in this book. (As I have been doing right along) may I make an aside? (An aside is a part in an old-time play or movie in which an actor steps out of character to say something to the audience of a semi-private or semi-confidential nature about the play.) I am confounded, and somewhat appalled when I read over the scholarly works referred to, about the Astral Light, and about the Gnostic Demiurge, and, last read, about Mithra, and realize how close these people were to Great Truths — only one step more — the Great Truth — that I have been pursuing down "backwards," being unable to perceive it "forwards" as is usual with me.

The Great Truth, the one step more, to be very exact, is the Control of Physical Matter.

Now, it could be that their ancient worthies *did* make that *last step*, but never recorded it down on a written record (not many people could read and write in those days), OR maybe as soon as it dawned on an individual what a Power he had acquired maybe he just disappeared, or at least shut up, and how can disappearances, or silence, be traced at this date, 2,000 to 3,000 years later? Also, as I said before, and will say again, the modern historical scholar, the historian, are not looking for Occult happenings, or anything like that, and so we Occultists will look in vain for evidence of discovery/development/use of Occult matters in the histories of Mithra, and the Gnostics, and related societies and religions in ancient times. End of Aside.

To return to the Gnostics and some of their teachings. THEY said that man had the possibility of escape from this Physical Plane "mess" through Knowledge (or wisdom) (Sophia — Greek word) or, rather, Man could acquire the Power to bring order, ORDER, out of the usual Physical Plane confusion by acquiring Knowledge (I feel sure they meant that Knowledge leads to Wisdom).

Some further information, from Gnostic sources, gives a pattern of ideas which ideas are more or less in accord with basic systems of Universal construction — such as the idea that a "piece" of GOD "came down from above" and got itself enmeshed in Matter — sometimes referred to as "seven layers or coverings of matter" — corresponding to the seven planetary "Gods" and "Goddesses," five male and two female. This "piece" of God is also called the/a spark, or as others put it, the/a Divine Spark, which Divine Spark apparently IS YOU-NOW, how we got "this way (the way you and I are now) I don't know, and neither does anyone else." (Later I'll try and connect up the preceding ideas with another set of similar ideas from another source, and hopefully the connection will cast more light on it).

But the Gnostics said, I repeat, that the way "out" was through Knowledge. I suppose it means self-knowledge, or Knowledge of Self.

I am going to bring this section to a close. I, and now you, are out on the fringes of the Great Unknown (big deal), and we are more or less on our own. I wish I could find *Definite confirmation* in some already written book (not hints, but DEFINITE CONFIRMATION) so I didn't have to mill about in this manner, BUT don't be discouraged. *YOU do have a THING that does work*, and that is the basic-basic-basic knowledge I have given here; that the Physical Plane is run-managed-governed by a half-God called the demi-urge, and *there is every possibility that KNOWLEDGE (already given) can bring you to* "him"/"it" *and you can influence* "him"/"it," which is certainly something greatly to be desired above Gold and Jewels!! I mean that the Knowledge I have already given you in my book, "The Art and Practice of Getting Material Things Through Creative Visualization," *does work*!! Go to it.

Chapter 8

Elsewhere, I made a reference to a Jewish scholar whom I met through others. He is a man of wide Catholic (not Roman Catholic) tastes, and interests, a very capable mind, which apparently has a ready language getting ability, so that he not only has the Hebrew, modern and ancient, but also the Arabic, as well as the Hindu Sanskrit. And, he appears to have covered the top, inner secret religious writings, in each of these three fountainheads of religion, and he further states he found correlations in these "tops" which made them all the same ideas, basically.

Apart from these religious matters, he seems to be a physical scientist, and is presently working on a new type of seismograph that, I hope, will predict earthquakes in advance, although he didn't say that positively.

He claims to have used the Knowledge about Yod-Heh-Vav-Heh to bring himself wealth, and I do know he owns two houses right in the middle of a quite expensive district here in Los Angeles.

He himself is too much of a non-crusader to gather this stuff together and give it to you to help you in your life struggle, although he will talk to people about these subjects if they come to him, but not in large numbers. I would say that this material is too ephemeral for most students. Personally, I found his material much too stiff for me, and I have to confine myself to asking him specific questions, and then attempting to untangle something from the answers, which can be used practically.

The following is the gist of the material I got from him about aspects of the Higher, Inner Jewish Doctrine:

There IS the/a vast countenance called the Arik Anpin, the lesser countenance called Zoar Anpin. The Vast

Countenance just does nothing, stands/sits "there" and watches the lesser Countenance. The lesser countenance DREAMS this Universe along in a continuous dream (Dion Fortune said that this Physical Plane World was a thought-form projection, being projected by (some, a) God.) Thus, you could say that the lesser countenance creates this world, which is somewhat analogous to the actions of the Demiurge, when it was said that the Demi-urge "dealt" with the physical plane, acted/was the "agent" of the non-physical God in dealing with the physical plane, which physical plane could never, by the very nature of its be-ing, be contacted by the non-physical God in any way.

Also, I want to add here that I found that there was a group of Gnostics who taught the above somewhat differently. They said the Demiurge, instead of being an agent, as stated before, was a creator, who created this Physical World!!! (As, indeed, he/it MIGHT have done at the order of the non-physical God, who, even though non-physical, can dream, can't he?)

Well!! Exactly what may be the answer to the above puzzle? THE JOB YOU HAVE IS TO FIND OUT HOW TO INFLUENCE WHAT'S-HIS-NAME, and that is possible, and that is your job — and that is what Magic is. So Be It. Amen.

Chapter 9

As this book is about the Caballa, more especially the Tree of Life Caballa, we can now return to that part — The Tree of Life.

We had previously "Pillars of the Tree" and their relation to the present, past, and future, which you can review again if you do not clearly remember it.

Also, in the last chapter I made a reference to the Raw God Force, and also referred to a necessary contacting of the Force through a "veil" or filter of some kind or, to use a lower down material term, a modifier of some kind. A modifier which will tame down the raw violent God Force so that we fragile shells can come as close to the source of power as we can and influence the Power in our favor, or to use a terminology we studied before, to influence the Dream of Physical Plane Existence of the Lesser Countenance Dreamer in our favor.

Or, to use the still other terminology from the Hindu sources — the concept of the Astral Light or, Akasha, in which all things are and from which all things come (very much the same idea as the concept of the Dreamer in many ways).

The only difference being that the Akasha, while being thought of as having all things in it in potential, was not considered as doing any actual dreaming about those things. Creative Morning Dreaming.

We will leave these higher conceptions for now. Indeed, I had not intended for them to be in this book, nor had I intended to go as far into the Raw God Energy Creation Force. This Raw God Energy Creation Source came in here because it was just at this time that we came across a new source of knowledge.

This new source of Knowledge is, however, very cranky to manage. It has all this Knowledge information, but it is all jumbled up and divided between Jewish sources, Hindu sources, and now I find that it has equated a lot with the Koran!! It has to be handled carefully, and as I said this is all I have for now. When I have more, I will give it out, but some of the highest will have to go into the "Secret" book for the reasons heretofore given.

Therefore, in this book we will return to the place where I first mentioned the two countenances and the Astral Light, and take it from there.

The Astral Light you will encounter and "see" on the Inner Plane is the Demiurge, but as I said before, the Half-God Agent in a raw or crude form and, like all things in a raw or crude for, the material must be altered before it can be used. This analogy also seems to be true of the Astral Light, the raw Astral Light Material (it occurs to me that another name I heard Dion Fortune us — Undifferentiated Elemental Substance — is also applicable here to the Raw Astral Light).

Therefore, to use the same name — Undifferentiated Elemental Substance reference — The Raw Astral Light should become separated into component parts by a symbolic filter or prism and the component parts used separately by each of you for its designated purpose.

The Filter, or prism, is analogous to the Tree of Life pattern, the Sephiroth, the Minor Arcana, and the Major Arcana — the paths between the Sephiroth.

These three things tone down and split up and designate the Raw Astral Light into useable forms — Forces.

All the myriad activities of our physical plane are divided up and ruled, governed, by: (1) Astrological Forces; (2) Planetary Forces; (3) The Four Elemental Forces, and these signals and signs, etc.

Note: We will proceed in the text along the lines of the toned down Forces, and you must throw yourself, for now, into the ordinary use of these toned down Forces, but with more power and drive, now that you know more about them and what you are doing. BUT there is the future development possibilities beckoning, of dealing correctly and safely with the Raw Astral Light.

Now, for God's sake, don't be suggestive or swayed by my statements, or feel that because I experienced so and so you should have to also. Not so. But I will tell you about the following: The first time I realized the true nature of the white light I had seen in my ordinary dreams, I approached it on the inner plane and attempted to contact/influence it. I did get a reaction — undesirable but plain. No hurt, but it did have an impact on me. I stayed in bed two days, while I thought the matter over and came to the conclusion that it was not a simple matter to contact and influence the Raw Astral Light Force.

Now, my then assistant secretary, exploring along somewhat the same lines, the Jewish concept of the lesser countenance, the Dreamer, came into the same knockout condition, too, and was laid out for several days and, for several days, was quite dull.

Now, to return to the prism, filter, transformer, or even rectifier, to give it another name for a cosmic device to reduce the Raw Astral Light — Akasha — The Dream of the lesser countenance Dreamer, to manageable proportions — lowering the Raw Force down to more simple daily use levels.

As of this moment of writing, I have no idea how the Gods came into being, but evidently there was some discovery made eons ago by some sensitive person that something was out there, and acted like a shield against the blast of raw force, which raw force seemed everywhere and was everywhere, as my assistant found, but found in another manner, that is, discovered through a suggestion coming from and through my work on Astral Projection.

In the following pages I am going to reproduce a number of diagrams of the Tree of Life. Some of these diagrams will have familiar connections with each Sephiroth. Other diagrams will have connections that I have discovered myself; convictions that I have found nowhere else, and have come from my own inner consciousness.

Some of these convictions were given partly before in my book, "The Art and Practice of the Occult." I did not hold the newer stuff back when I wrote that book; I just didn't have it then. I'm concerned that this knowledge seems to come in jolts and jerks, and not all at once. It seems that in order to advance I have to accumulate some more data in which is hidden something that sets me off again, and I go through another Gyration, a mental gyration, out of which comes a burst of new knowledge. I wish it would all come at once, for your sake as well as mine.

As I said, in the coming diagrams I am going to place these God/Goddess transformers on the Tree one by one, and explain their functions in descending order. I will also attempt to explain how to use these God and Goddesses, but I feel as I write this book, that this section might prove too long and not adaptable to all students, so I may have to make that working section up separately. I will, however, give all that space allows here, and what I do give here should be enough for any of your ordinary life's needs, at least during the first part of your occult work.

Therefore, I begin another chapter, starting with the basic of basics, but which will have no end, because there is no end to TRUTH.

The beginning of IT ALL. Note: Although in this chapter we are going to explain the frontiers of the Occult and to get into some mighty fine splits of matter, and some very thin non-physical aspects of higher, more ephemeral matter status, REMEMBER the whole total of all operations have to be grounded in Malkuth finally, to be of any value to us, and that I will endeavor to show you. In other words, the object of all occult work is to refine and enhance matter, and help your physical well-being, at least at first.

If there is anything that makes the blood dry up in my veins, it is the Theosophical, cum Alice Bailey, cum India, cum Buddah stuff about "Spiritual Development" (what is that?), which is not to be used for anything except higher things while, as I said elsewhere before, we starve to death gracefully on the physical plane!!

In the history of the United States a great to do was made about the disappearance of the physical Frontier in the West and its effect on American daily life. Then, during the great depression of the thirties, some cry was made that there was no wild frontier left to immigrate to and start life anew, etc. WELL, I now know, and state, that when I had the strong urge to explore the Inner Plane projection idea about ten years ago, I had no clear idea of what the main motive was to be. Now I'm beginning to see some light and motive along the way. It looks as though, to continue my work, everyone interested will have to explore the inner plane and integrate the power potentialities. You must bring the Inner Planes World operations and functions into your personal life, and living thus INCREASED.

NOW ATTENTION!!! The above-described living has nothing to do with the moans and groans of those enemies of Occult Teaching who are constantly worried that the Occult will be used for wrong purposes.

This new concept, which I here present, is not any dabbling in the Occult. It is a reaching into a new different life entirely. A life embracing and growing into another expanded concept, embracing the physical mechanisms for use down here on this plane. Please remember that I said before that each plane was governed by rules and laws that were made on the plane above it.

So, to go to the above is what we are after, and please don't lose sight of this goal.

So, now I have to make a little review. I am trying to show the way that the raw undifferentiated elemental essence — the Astral Light — the Sun behind the Sun and the lesser countenance who dreams this dream into existence. As this raw substance comes down the Tree of Life planes, the various transformers, the prisms, it goes through, changes and modifies the Raw Substance and separates it into its component parts, which components you can handle in the separated form. Study the diagram already given.

Above the Sephiroth #1 there is what Dion Fortune called the negative veils of existence. And, then goes on and does not explain what they are, much less how they are to be used.

I do not know what the Negative Veils of Existence are, and in all probability we will not have to concern ourselves with them for eons to come.

The first Sephiroth is called Kether, which means Crown. As I said before Dion Fortune gives a whole group of attributes and symbols to this Sephiroth, and to each of the others to follow. You, in all probability, should get Dion Fortune's book, "The Mystical Qabalah," and study it carefully. I myself didn't find the Jewish symbols too illuminating, and then next, some Egyptian, but the Egyptian is so old that it is hard to make modern connection, as the Egyptians didn't stress the aspects of life that we do, and that the Greeks did. We still follow these aspects to some extent, so the Greek is somewhat familiar to us.

To continue then along with the Greek system of God and Goddesses and their attributes, through which the raw astral light becomes refined and differentiated into useable form. Or, shall we use the overworked term, vibrations or vibes? Consider it done.

Consulting your sample Tree of Life, please remember that Dion Fortune's descriptions pertain to the beginning of the creation of this Physical Universe, whereas what we are considering her in this book is the continuing of an already created universe, with you arriving on the scene some billions of years later, and ready and willing to take up your part in a going concern.

So, in the process of creating the Universe, the first Sephiroth overflowed and created the second Sephiroth, named Chokmah, or Zodiac, or Space, to operate in, space to function in.

There are no Gods attached to Chokmah (there is a God name-Almighty God — El — or Al). The Astral Light is spreading out to operate. Next, we come to the third Sephiroth, Binah, and here the first of the Greek Pantheon appears. The God Saturn, or to say it in the form we are studying in this book. Here in Binah appears the first prism and/or transformer which modifies or steps down the Raw Astral Light into useable form, governing certain physical Plane objects.

The list of physical plane objects governed by Saturn are as follows, but not necessarily complete: Coal mines, oil wells, all mines, forests, old people, old plans, wills, antiques, all old things, wood products, paper, but not what is written on it, metal, lead, and old books.

Notice — I said above, governing certain — etc. I may as well add here that while I used the word govern, it is also true that the physical things themselves are made out of the Astral Light itself. The reason I used the word govern is that I am still enmeshed in the old ideas of differences between forces and things, or the world's idea of separation of things. Can you, will you, take this next step and drop the idea of separations? Try!!

Dear students, another note. At this point another vast branch of directions comes up. I must choose between the line I am pursuing, the steeping down line, or turn aside for this different line. The line is how the Astral Light changes itself as Light into solid things, through the medium of the five elemental forces or the physical plane. I cannot handle this here. I must leave it for another book, perhaps even the secret book, to prevent misuse. We will return to the transforming-down-line-knowledge of the Astral Light.

Saturn is the first unchangeable recognizable God you will find on the Tree of Life on the way down from above.

Please get a good college textbook on Mythology. The one by Gayley, recommended in this book, is quite good. Read all it says about Saturn. Much of what it will say will not make everyday sense to you, but do remember it is a Myth telling a story. And, then you remember what the writer of the book didn't know, but what you know about Saturn being a step-down transformer, transforming the Raw God material into useable forms. Forms to be used by you. (Again, I feel I have to put a note in here about that subject!!) Who are? In relation to all this? As this is what we are talking about now, I can't do the lines at once. So, the second line, "Who are you?" will have to wait until the next, or maybe the secret book. So, back to the God forms to be used by you. There is another matter here that I feel should be taken care of before we go on. It is the matter of the worship of the Gods of the Greek Pantheon.

Those of you who come from Christian churches might be troubled at the idea of conflict with the first and second commandments about worshipping other Gods. You are not worshipping other, different, Gods. (All Gods and Goddesses are the same.) In using these these God Forces, or focal points, you are not worshipping them, so be at ease about that.

Actually, you can easily understand that a God Form attached to a certain Sephiroth has a double function. The God Form must receive from above and transmit down to below. This double function was shown by giving the God a wife, a female who performed the negative receptive function of receiving the Raw Power from above, and then her husband took over and transmitted the Power along on below. As Dion Fortune said somewhere, "Each Sephipah is negative — receptive to above and, positive to below, or female-receptive to above, and male-positive, transmitting to below. Sometimes the receptive female was designated as a sister, and sometimes even brother and sister married. This goes to show that the story was clearly a legend — myth. The brother-sister marriage generally meant that there was no female of equal rank available to be a wife, in the case of the myth story being told — illustrated — so a sister of equal rank had to serve. Of course, as these Gods and Goddesses never existed physically on the physical plane, the brother-sister relationship is to be looked at as an illustration only, and not imitated down here.

There is another goddess whose station is here in Binah, whom you should know about and give definitive attention to, attention over and above what I can give you here.

Isis is definitely a type of female Saturn. As Saturn is the Father of all the Gods, so Isis is the Mother of, not only the Gods, but of all. All there is. All that exists.

I cannot go farther into Isis here, much as I would like to, because as I said, the Egyptian religion is so much the older than the Greek, which is nearer to us time-wise, that their objectives were entirely different than ours. While all Gods are the same, the Egyptians stressed much different aspects and goals. Not at all what we expect our Gods to bring to us today.

Before I leave Isis and proceed with the main theme of this book I will tell you a story.

I have always been partial to Isis, ever since I first heard of the Goddess, and I fancy I could say I developed a certain rapport with her. Perhaps in a past incarnation I was a priest of Isis. I used to attend a simple little church, and one Sunday morning they announced a solo, Gounod's "Ave Maria." As I have no use for Holy Mary as such, I slumped in the seat and went into a reverie. In my meditation reverie I contemplated the Mary-maria-sea, and it occurred to me that Mary was Isis as she is. My mental pictures then came to Egyptian Wall paintings of Isis, and as I was watching the wall painting — IT MOVED, TURNED AWAY FROM THE WALL AND LOOKED AT ME. This was so unexpected, and I was so surprised, that I woke up and stopped the vision. I will do this again and be prepared this time. And, so you can do this and more.

Now, with these little side issues out of the way we can go on with the main theme of the book.

Saturn, plus Isis, are the first practical step-down-transformers of the Astral Light Power, from the Raw state into the useful state on this physical plane. Note: you should have read my book, "The Art and Practice of the Occult," first or along with this book. Recall the additional knowledge about the Tree of Life, and the Past, Present, and Future given there. Also, the other additional knowledge about the Elemental Forces on the Sephiroth in their compound states. Of course, there is the existence of the Sephiroth Chokmah. I did not mean to jump over this Sephiroth, or leave it out, but the objects it rules are quite a little bit out of the ordinary individual's range. They are: radio, television, movies, electric power in the case of transmission of same, static electricity and its industrial uses, such as precipitators of dust, etc., magnetism in high concentrations, such as magnetism in "200+" machine coils, wherein electric currents run on endlessly, having no resistance, advanced type rockets, possibly fireworks, and personal extra sensory perception in connection with the psychic soul (whatever that is), travel to higher planes wherein there are no forms left, and only emotions exist, some kinds of fiction and plays, and again, I say these things are a little out of the ordinary person's use and contact. At first I had intended to mention them later, but it had been called to my attention that this out-of-place idea might be confusing.

Everything, anything, all things, all different things, each and every one of every kind of different thing on this Physical Plane is connected directly with a step-down transformer. One of the ten step-down transformers on the Tree of Life, seven Sephiroth of which are connected with the names of well-known Gods and Goddesses, and the other three Sephiroth are connected with the names and forces which are not as well known to the average person.

Kether, Chokmah, and Malkuth. Kether and Chokmah were given already. The powers of Malkuth are: Pan, male; Demeter, female; Persephone, Demeter's daughter; Baachus, Roman; and Osiris. There are others, but you link them up yourself.

SO THEN. As we make this journey through this rocky road of life, it would seem as though we were left defenseless to face all the enemies alone. But it isn't really. Through Knowledge you now know of the existence of the Astral Light. Through practice you can attain to seeing it, and once you have seen it for sure, you can try and work with it. And, when you can work it and/or work with it, you are on your way to Mastery over it all.

Chapter 10

As I progress in the writing of this book I am more and more convinced that I should put the WORKINGS of this Knowledge into a separate book, and make that book not too accessible.

Now, for God's sake, accuse me of anything, but don't accuse me of selling, just for more money, the Working Knowledge!!!

There are a number of reasons WHY the holdback above seems a good idea: (1) This knowledge is very valuable, and should be kept not common, for as soon as any Knowledge becomes common Knowledge the tendency is to belittle it, especially by those not ready, and that belittling would bother me no end. I have had a radio station man say to me in a loud accusing voice/manner, "I DON'T UNDERSTAND your books!" So, what the hell! He didn't understand them! So work on them! Study them! Absorb them! And, in the meanwhile, keep your ignorant mouth shut up!!! There is no way I can chop their heads open and pour in the Knowledge/Understanding, or give them the Knowledge in a pill they can swallow! (2) By the time you are ready for the Knowledge either one of two things should have happened: (a) you should understand IT yourself, or (b) be able, through Creative Visualization, to have brought you the *means*, the financial means, to have gotten you the *Working Knowledge* EASILY.

Dear Students: if neither one of these events have happened in your life, then you are not ready YET, but can be, so don't be upset, just work and study like fury (as I did), and you'll get all you can handle. Nothing can keep it from you when you are ready (so work like, as I did). Another thought — If I should put ALL THE WORKING

KNOWLEDGE DOWN HERE (I repeat), and many are not ready, the Knowledge would be screwed up, or half understood, or ignored, unrecognized. This does not seem proper, as I want you to have this knowledge and USE this Knowledge. Amen. Ah-men.

I will continue with more Knowledge. Put it this way: Your inner perceptions are growing all the time, and every time you read this Knowledge your inner perceptions grow more. It is possible you will never need any advanced Knowledge from me at all. So be it. But if you do, you do have the means already in your possession, through my book named, "The Art and Practice of Getting Material Things Through Creative Visualization," to bring you what you need, NOW.

There is another point which has now come up in the course of resolving this "different Knowledge conception" into working rules, which is, viz: The Gnostic ideas seem to have underlying them a note of negativeness and anxiety about "escaping" from this matter plane, and the other matter planes, and returning forthwith to the FATHER in the Kingdom of Light as quickly as possible, and with great dispatch, saying nothing about conquering these outer, other planes, or learning, or gaining anything at all in this process.

I wonder if this Gnostic, negative attitude towards this Physical World is not that which became the Christian Church's attitude, too, towards the material world as a "vale of tears." This, during the first four hundred years before Augustine promulgated his creed about original sin in the Garden of Eden, and so forth.

At the risk of boring you to tears, I wonder if, during the four hundred-year period until Augustine, the original ideas of Mithra and the Demiurgeous, who were sort of mediators between God and Man, as you will note if you read over their functions at all carefully, were changed by a process of human ignorance and a desire to simplify, into the basic Jesus Christ idea. All during this time period stories were circulating among the ignorant about the/a

God mediator which gradually got built up into a story of a virgin birth, a star, angels appearing to shepherds, etc., etc. (Mithra was born of a Virgin, a star appeared at his birth, angels appeared to some shepherds at night, etc., etc.)

Then appears a story by a Roman named Mark (Marcus) telling about a man-type saviour, followed by expansion of the story by an unknown named Matthew, followed by another, still late, expansion by another named Luke. Then came a very mysterious "gospel" by another unknown called John who expounded in very suspiciously Gnostic-type statements, which became less and less understood as the main story became more and more material in form and legend, and dumber and bigger dumbers, latched onto it. Also, at this same time, endless "books" appeared, Gospels and Revelations, and multiplied like mad. You'll find all this history in history. Look it up yourself. But, as I said, I just wondered: did the non-material concepts of Mithra and Gnosis and the Demiurgeous become a man/God saviour through the alchemy of Time, plus ignorance?

Whereas, I seem to detect in the Hebrew concepts of the Vast Countenance, and Lesser Countenance a degree of attainment to be gained through all this, attainment which was not there *"before,"* or perhaps I just read this into the writings of Dion Fortune, where she said that we should round the outer buoy of the nader of matter, as a yacht must turn the outer most marking buoy in a race, before trying to cut short our sojourn here on this material plane.

It would seem to me that we should "escape" this matter plane through a combination of Knowledge, which should lead to a mastery of matter, before we "leave" it and "return" to the place of all Light, and not just flee from matter by a series of tricks, magical tricks, which do nothing for matter. Question: does matter deserve any consideration? What is your opinion?

So now, with that out of the way we can proceed to the next outlay of Knowledge, or shall we call it the next outburst of Knowledge?

I am going to proceed with the Knowledge on the

assumption that WE are to conquer/control matter and thus "escape" its thrall.

As far as I have gone into the Gnostic and the Hebrew ideas of the Countenance creation and existence of the Material World, I have not run across anything pertaining to the actual building blocks of the Material Plane, or rather I haven't run across the building blocks of the Material Plane in any form I recognize as yet, unless it is hidden from me, or us, in some way, or unless that is the "secret part" they are hiding from us. Or what?

I will have to turn to Hindu sources for the following Knowledge, which, for some reason is plainly given more or less there, but again not connected with still other Knowledge available in Gnostic and Hebrew sources. There is an old book, 1887, of which there are many secondhand copies around, named "Nature's Finer Forces," by Rama Prasad, and printed by The Theosophical Publishing House at Adyar, Madras, India, and distributed by the Theosophical Press at Wheaton, Illinois. You should get yourself a copy of this book and keep studying it from now on, as it is quite deep, although I found the Hindu names of things a little trying, maybe you'll like them better than I did.

I sat here for ten minutes cognizing as to how to set up this section for clear understanding. Understanding of the building blocks of the material universe, which the World-Builder uses to create a material world, which he/it can never KNOW, in he/its original existence condition, that is, until he/it divides he/it into individual divine sparks and "descends/falls/pushes" himself/itself down into his/its own creation, and then fights/struggles to get "back up" again, presumably additionally enriched by the experience.

No human being down here knows if the above is true or not, but I shall be very greatly astounded if something very similar to this is not true, otherwise we have a very screwy universe setup. Well!!! There still are certain things which do WORK here, which I have given you — so work from the bottom up, but study the following as a theory, which change or modify as becomes clearer, as time goes on.

I will try to describe an ancient statue/carving/symbol, and in explaining this statue/carving/symbol will cover the field of the Forces which are the building blocks of the Physical Universe, which Knowledge should enable you to understand them and use them and not they use you.

Please try to picture the figure designated.

To start, the center is a male figure, nude. The feet of this figure are hooves of an animal. Wrapped around the figure are the coils of a snake, or probably more artistically known as a serpent. The figure has wings. The figure has a lion's head on the body opposite the "solar plexus" opposite the heart.

The figure has, in its left hand, a large staff, and in its right hand a bundle of something that I am not able to make out from the reproduction I have seen exactly what it is. It does resemble some flames at one end; also, flames seem to be coming from back of the head.

The figure is surrounded by an oval circle containing the signs of the Zodiac. If you examine the other examples, you will find more or less the same symbols; some have more symbol, and some have less symbol.

Please remember two things at this point in our studies: (1) The originators of this carving symbol on a wall in a Mithra Temple did not know as much background Occult Metaphysics as you do now, and (2) the originators did not know of the coming cross connections with the Gnostics, as you will know from your history reading as we progress.

Also, by no means last or least here, in this book we are hunting for clues to the existence AND USE of the Astral Light in our daily lives. A use which it is doubtful that the worshippers/devotees of Mithra were looking for or had the basic full information on.

Hence, the basic meaning of this symbol was — the man-like figure is YOU, the unseen YOU. You are surrounded by all the Forces pictured there in the symbol and up to now partly pointed out and explained.

All the Forces symbolized by those symbols are adaptations, and combinations of the Astral Light REACTING upon, and recombining with each other. (I seem to be a little disorderly here, and out of ordered sequence, but the Astral Light — the Demiurge — who is probably Mithra, too, under another guise, is not too easy to expound), constitute the Physical World Plane.

It would seem as if this Plane holds YOU captive, and, I guess you can say for practical reasons, the Physical Plane does hold YOU/ME/US captive. But it is also logically true that Knowledge/Wisdom (Sophia) does open the WAY OUT. (I repeat) You ARE the Demiurge and Mithra in some heretofore secret way and connected to them.

To resume, in the symbol there are evidences of the Astral Light showing all over the symbol. The Astral Light was actually a fourfold Creation Force; fivefold if you consider Akasha as one of the Forces. Akasha is one of the hardest to understand, hence least understood of the five Elemental Forces, which constitute the Hindu form/name of the Astral Light, which the Hindu call Prana. (We may go into this more later, if not more in this book, then in another book. Some of this has already been treated in other books.)

The evidences of the Four Elemental Forces in the symbol are: the figure has wings. Wings are the symbol of Air, the Elemental Force of Air. There are several Fire symbols; flame above the head, I think flames in the hand, and the Lion head opposite the solar plexus is also a symbol of the Elemental Force of Fire. The Elemental Force of Earth is shown in the bull hooves of this figure. I am unable to recognize the symbol for the Elemental Force of Water, for which I apologize, but please don't let it upset the symbolism, as Water IS THERE. Taurus and Libra are ruled by Venus, which is Water of Water (see the book, "The Art and Practice of The Occult"). Also, Cancer is considered a Water sign, along with Scorpio and Aquarius. But, I will agree, there should be a Water Elemental Force symbol somewhere on the figure, but unless it is connected with the snake, I cannot find it in my picture here. I will make enquiries about it, but as the Mithra priests, and Gnostic

Priests have been gone from this earth plane for about 2,000 years, I hardly know where to turn for information!!!

The snake ascending the figure's body in five loops is said to be the raising Kundalini Fire, and this ascension has to do with the increasing "spiritualization" of the man figure (which, of course, is you).

Here, at this point, is one of those tricks, deceptions, dead ends, and riddles which abound in the Occult. This matter has been treated elsewhere in other books, and writings, to which I refer you, but I will cover some of the ground here again.

In the first place, between this Earth Plane and the Etheric Plane there seems to be a well-defined *"reversal"* pattern. What is coming "here" is going "there." Man is upside down, end for end, reversed to the Etheric Plane. Therefore, this Force is not in reality ascending — it is descending!!

REFERENCES

Dion Fortune   Mystical Qabalah
Cosmic Doctrine
Practical Occultism
   in Daily Life
Psychic Self-Defense

"Fiction"   Secrets of Dr. Taverner
Demon Lover
Winged Bull
Sea Priestess
Moon Magic

Dr. F. I. Regardie   The Tree of Life
The Middle Pillar
A Garden of Pomegranates
The Golden Dawn

Aleister Crowley   Qabalah of Aleister Crowley (777)

William Gray   The Ladder of Lights
The Office of the Holy Tree

MacGregor Mathers   The Kabbalah Unveiled

Gayley   Classic Myths in
    Literature and Art

A letter to Ophiel at the address below will bring you up to date on new material, including possible classes on the Occult.

Ophiel is unable to answer letters in detail now due to things, not the least of which is old age. But he'll keep on trying.

Note: Please don't send special delivery letters or registered letters as it takes ten time longer for me to get them than it does for ordinary mail.

Ophiel

950 Larkspur Drive
Oakland, California   94610